Sally Featherstone and Su Wall

Sounds

Fun

0–20 months

Published 2010 by A&C Black Publishers Limited
36 Soho Square, London, W1D 3QY
www.acblack.com

ISBN 978-1-4081-1490-2

Written by Sally Featherstone and Su Wall
Design by Trudi Webb
Photographs © Shutterstock, Fotolia and Rebecca Skerne

With thanks to the following schools for their help with the photos:
Valley Children's Centre (Rotherham) and Yarm Preparatory School (Stockton-on-Tees)

Printed in Great Britain by Latimer Trend & Company Limited

A CIP record for this publication is available from the British Library.

To see our full range of titles
Visit www.acblack.com/featherstone

Contents

Introduction

The best environment for communication

It is now well known that communication skills such as eye contact, body language, listening and speaking are at the heart of all learning and development. Children with good communication skills grow up to be confident members of society, who can use their skills to make the most of life inside and out of the education system. We also know that babies and children who, for various reasons, do not develop these skills in early childhood are at risk throughout the rest of their lives. They may fail to make strong relationships with others, they may be less successful in their working lives, and find learning much more difficult.

Such knowledge about language development has resulted in government initiatives such as *Every Child a Talker, Communication Matters* and *Letters and Sounds*, which are intended to support practitioners as they work with babies and children in the ever-increasing range of childcare provision. Some babies and children now spend more time in day - care than they do at home, so the role of practitioners in supporting language development is very important, not just for those children growing up in disadvantaged or lone parent families, but those where both parents work long hours, where the home language is not English, or where the many other pressures of modern life mean that families spend less time together.

While the environment for communication in the early years should ideally replicate the best home situation, there are some factors which practitioners in settings may need to take into account when evaluating their own settings. The impact of radio, television, computers, mobile phones and constant background music has had a significant effect on children's ability to listen, speak and concentrate.

- Practitioners should be aware of these features of home life and restrict the use of television and computers in their setting as much as possible. In fact, many experts say that babies and children should have little or no television or computer exposure until they are three years old. This ideal is perhaps unrealistic in children's home lives, but we should make every effort to counteract this in early years settings.
- Mobile phones, computer games and MP3 players are solitary occupations, often without the involvement of another person, and certainly without the added messages of eye contact, facial expression and body language. Practitioners should bare in mind that the parent who spends much of their time texting or listening to their iPod will not be communicating as much with their child.
- Background music from the radio or television disrupts attention and restricts hearing. Music is a useful tool for practitioners but it should not be used indiscriminately. Keep music at a suitable volume and for particular activities —don't use it as 'aural wallpaper'!

Dummies and pacifiers

Dummies and pacifiers can also be very damaging to language development, particularly when they are used all day. This use restricts the development of speech by reducing the muscular development within the mouth and tongue, as well as endangering the formation of teeth. Practitioners will need to handle this information sensitively when talking to parents, and encourage them to restrict the use of dummies and pacifiers to sleep time or when the child is distressed. Children who crawl, walk or run around with a dummy or feeding cup constantly in their mouth endanger their language development and may endanger their personal safety if they fall. Settings should consider whether to include guidance on dummies, pacifiers and feeding cups in their policies and procedures as well as in their prospectus or guidance to parents.

The role of the Key Person in communication

The role of key person is vital to the success of *Sounds Fun* activities. Close bonding between key adults and the babies and children in your setting will create a firm foundation for language development. Key members of staff know each child and their family well, and they are in a unique position to nurture language and social development. Their observations will be vital in deciding which activities to plan for the child, and they can create the warm, welcoming and informed link with the child's family.

The key child or key group is at the heart of these activities. They are ideal for key group times, so build them into your daily programme, using individual and small group times for talking, listening, singing and rhymes. Create comfortable places indoors and outside for these key times – settees, armchairs, swing seats, garden benches, bean bags, cushions and rugs are all useful places for language activities where babies and children feel at ease.

Remember that the language you use is crucial to babies' and children's own language development. Use appropriate language whenever you are with children, even if you think they can't hear or are not listening. Children are like sponges and they will soak up your language, whoever you are talking to, and whatever they appear to be doing at the time.

Some tips are:

- If you use 'baby language' such as 'baa-lamb', 'moo-cow' or 'quack-quack' you will restrict children's language development. As a professional you need to help children to learn and use the proper names for animals and objects.
- Don't use slang or 'street language', and discourage others in your setting from using it too. You may need to discuss this as a group and even decide which words are unsuitable. We sometimes use unsuitable words without thinking, and are surprised when children repeat them back to us, or use them in their play.
- Local words or dialect words are part of children's world, but you do need to help them to use a range of words, including alternatives to the local ones.

Introduction

Children with additional needs

As Key person you have a responsibility to identify, and if necessary seek help for, children with additional needs. Your setting will have a policy for the support of these children, and if you observe extreme difficulties you should follow the procedures in the policy.

However, some babies and children have developmental delays, which are less severe and can be supported by adapting the activities to make them simpler or less demanding. Other options include choosing activities from an earlier book, or limiting the length of time or the size of the group for the activities you choose. Observation, note-taking and consultation with colleagues and parents will help you to get the right match of activity for each child.

Taking the activities outside

Some children love being outside, are naturally more focused there, and learn best in an outdoor environment, where the sounds, sights, colours and smells are so different from indoors. Outdoor play is now a requirement within the Early Years Foundation Stage, and we have supported this requirement by embedding outdoor activities in all four Sounds Fun books. Each activity in each book has suggestions for taking the idea out of doors, regardless of whether you have a large or small outdoor area.

Some settings have ideal outdoor spaces but of course some of you are providing outdoor experiences in gardens, parks, playgrounds, community spaces or even the balcony of your flat! These are all suitable places for taking 'Talking Time' out of doors and we hope you will adapt the suggestions to fit your own circumstances.

Of course, every setting has its own policies and procedures for outdoor play, and we would strongly advise that you continue to follow these, as every setting is different. However, we would like to add some specific guidance for the 'Talking Time' activities, which we hope will help you to make the most of your outdoor area. Your outdoor area should include spaces for stillness and quiet reflection, away from the busy bikes and ball play. These places could include seats and benches, grassy areas, pop-up tents and other shelters, blankets, mats, cushions, sleeping bags, groundsheets or mattresses. Use these areas for individual or small group times for talking, listening, story telling or singing, and be there in all weathers and during all four seasons. A Place to Talk Outside by Elizabeth Jarman (Featherstone) has some excellent ideas for making sure outdoor spaces are the kind of places young children will develop their language skills.

Involving parents

These books contain a wealth of suggestions for working with parents, and simple ideas for activities parents will be able to do to support their children's learning. The section 'Involving parents' included with each activity suggests things that parents can do at home, things they can bring to show at the setting and other ideas for simple home-based resources.

How will 'Sounds Fun' activities help you?

This series of books is intended to help you help children with sounds, words, talking and reading.

The activities:

- expand the work you are already doing in your own setting to ensure that every child becomes a confident talker and listener – with the best foundations for later speaking, listening, reading and writing;
- support your work with individual children and groups within the Key person process;
- help you in your work with parents, who are children's first and most influential educators;
- provide stimulating and varied activities, carefully matched to the developmental stages in your setting, from babies to children of Reception age, where the activities will be useful support for your phonics sessions.

Which age range are the activities suitable for?

Every activity is presented in the same format to make it easier for you to use within your own planning framework. For ease of use, we have divided the activities into four age ranges, covering the whole of the Early Years Foundation Stage:

- Book 1 covers developmental stages 1 and 2: babies from birth to 20 months (Babies)
- Book 2 covers developmental stages 3 and 4: babies and children from 16 to 36 months (Toddlers)
- Book 3 focuses on development stage 5: children from 30 50 months (Pre school)
- Book 4 focuses on development stage 6: children from 40 – 60+ months (Reception)

Of course, if you have children whose communication levels are high, you may want to dip into the next book in the series, and if you have children who have individual needs or would benefit from more reinforcement at an earlier stage, you can refer to earlier books.

What's inside each book?

Each book contains 35 activities, each on a double page spread and featuring:

- The focus activity (What you need, what you do and what you say);
- How you could **enhance** the activity by adding more or different resources;
- How you can **extend** the activity for older children or different sized groups;
- Taking the activity **outside** into your garden, a park or other play area;
- Suggestions for **songs, rhymes and stories**;
- **Key vocabulary and gestures** for you to use during the activity;
- Suggestions for **things to look for** as you observe the children during the activity (Look, listen and note);
- How to **use the activity with parents**, either by adapting for home use, or involving parents in your work in the setting.

Some activities will become favourites with the babies and children, and you will return to them again and again in your daily routine, building them into such times as snack, changing and rest times, as well as in the introduction to stories and song sessions.

Peek-a-boo!

This activity is suitable for one or two babies from birth to 9 months.

What you need:

A small blanket or piece of soft material, about the size of a tea towel

A warm, safe place

Bouncy chairs

A few baby toys such as rattles or soft toys

Enhancing the activity

- Choose some noisy toys to hide behind or under the blanket.
- Find different textured materials to hide behind and encourage the babies to explore the materials.
- Sing a song about the toy. Make it up if you can't remember one or use a nursery rhyme or your own words to a familiar tune such as: *Peek-a-boo, peek-a-boo, where are you?* to the tune of *'Peter Pointer, Peter Pointer where are you?'*
Older babies might enjoy 'Peek-a-boo' from *This Little Puffin* (Puffin Books)

Everybody enjoys playing 'peek-a-boo', especially young babies. It's a very easy activity that takes no preparation and can be done anywhere. It's a great way of forming relationships and communicating with babies from a very early age.

What you do

1 Place the bouncy chairs in a safe, warm place.
2 Talk to the babies as you gently put them into their bouncy chairs, saying 'Let's play peek-a-boo'.
3 Hold the blanket between you and the babies.
4 Talk to the babies, saying 'Where has (your name) gone?'
5 Bring the blanket down, saying 'Peek-a-boo, I can see you.'
6 Use plenty of facial expression and eye contact with the babies, emphasising your voice on 'peek-a-boo'.
7 Let them feel the blanket and encourage them to explore the texture with their fingers and toes. Older babies will reach out and pull the blanket to their face and mouth.
8 Repeat a couple of times, observing the babies' reactions.
9 Choose a toy and hold it near to the babies so they can see it (20 to 35 cm is a good distance).
10 Hide the toy behind the blanket and say, 'Where has the... gone?'
11 As you bring the blanket away from the toy say 'Lets find the... Peek-a-boo! Here it is'. If one of the babies reaches out for the toy, move it into contact with their fingers and hands, praising them for effort and talking about the texture and colour of the toy.
12 Follow the same process of hiding a variety of toys and yourself and keep praising the babies' responses.
13 Keep talking and playing 'peek-a-boo' while the babies are happy and involved. Don't go on too long!

Extending the challenge

- Play 'peek-a-boo' round the corner of furniture or the door.
- With older babies:
  - Let them hold the materials and encourage them to find the toys themselves.
  - Use a piece of transparent material and gently put it over the baby's head, letting him/her pull it off to play 'peek-a-boo' themselves.

Look, listen and note

Does the baby…
- *Focus on objects, and respond to different toys?*
- *Follow moving objects with his/her gaze (tracking)?*
- *Respond to sounds, songs and voices?*
- *Make sounds, bubbles or babbling noises?*
- *Grasp, kick or reach?*
- *Stay engaged? How long was his/her attention span?*
- *Smile and laugh to indicate he/she is enjoying the activity?*

Involving parents

You could…
- *Take some photos and display them, so parents can see how you do the activity.*
- *Demonstrate the activity.*

Key words and gestures

- Look
- Use of the baby's name
- Toy and object names
- Names of sounds
- Repeated sound and rhythmical phrases help babies language to develop
- Use gesture and facial expression to reinforce what you say: 'What's that?' 'Where have you gone?' 'Where is the rattle?' 'Is it hiding?' 'I can see you' 'Who's a clever boy?' 'Peek-a-boo' 'Can you see me?' 'What does the material feel like?' 'Is it soft, furry…?' 'Are you touching the material?' 'I can see your eyes' 'I can touch your face. Can you?'
- Keep your face where they can see you – you need to be quite close!

Take it outside

- Always check that babies lying on the ground are protected from the sun, from the damp and wind, from other children who may be playing nearby, and from insects and other wildlife.
- Put the bouncy chairs on a level surface in a shady, safe place on the grass or under a tree or bush, so they can also watch and listen to the leaves and the sounds while they play peek-a-boo.

TOP TIP
Be sensitive, play 'peek-a-boo' gently so you don't startle the babies.

Eye to eye

This activity is suitable for one baby from birth.

What you need:

Somewhere comfortable to sit

A warm quiet area with minimum disruptions

This is a lovely quiet time activity with a baby and is often one of the first 'conversations' that babies have with their carers/parents. Every baby needs plenty of these quiet conversations, as eye contact is essential to good communication skills.

What you do

1 Hold the baby with their head fully supported by your arm.
2 Ensure that the baby can gaze into your face with ease and can see you – 20 to 35 cm is a good distance.
3 Stand or sit where the light is falling on your face so they can see you easily.
4 Talk to the baby as you gently start to rock backwards and forwards maintaining eye contact as you do so.
5 Softly sing a lullaby or a nursery rhyme to the baby.
6 Use plenty of facial expression and eye contact with the baby and as you rock, remember time is needed to allow the baby to focus and follow.
7 Observe the baby's reactions and praise them when they respond through facial expression and movement of their hands and body.
8 When the baby smiles at you, smile back and praise them with a loving cuddle.

Enhancing the activity

- Use mirrors – see Mirror fun on page 14.
- Each time you feed and change the baby, talk to them about what you are doing.
- ♪ Sing any gentle songs and lullabies such as: *Hush a Bye Baby, Miss Polly* or *Twinkle, Twinkle*.

Key words and gestures

- Look
- Use of the baby's name
- Names of sounds
- Repeated sound and rhythmical phrases help babies' language to develop
- Use gesture and facial expression to reinforce what you say: 'What's that?' 'Where have you gone?' 'Where is the rattle?' 'Is it hiding?' 'I can see you' 'Who's a clever boy/girl?' 'Peek-a-boo' 'Can you see me?' 'What does the material feel like?' 'Is it soft, furry ...?' 'Are you touching the material?' 'I can see your eyes' 'I can touch your face' 'Can you?'
- Keep your face where they can see you – you need to be quite close!

TOP TIP
Talk to babies as much as you can!

Look, listen and note

Does the baby…
- *Follow your movements with his/her gaze (tracking)?*
- *Respond to sounds, songs and voices?*
- *Make sounds, bubbles and babbling noises?*
- *Reach out to touch your face, hands or fingers?*
- *Smile with enjoyment?*

Take it outside

- 'Eye to eye' is a lovely activity to do outside.
- Always check to be sure babies are protected from the sun, from the damp and wind, from other children who may be playing nearby, and from insects or other wildlife.
- Talk to the baby about the outdoor environment: 'Can you see the trees?' 'Hear the birds singing?' 'It's a lovely sunny day today.'

Extending the challenge

- Move around the room showing the baby the environment.
- Sit with two babies next to each other encouraging communication between you and the two babies.
- For older babies, let two or more babies communicate freely between themselves with close company of a familiar adult.

Involving parents

- *Remind parents that although the baby may not fully understand what you are saying, conversation is vital to stimulate the brain.*
- *Use every day occurrences to talk to the baby about what you are doing and what you can see.*

Let's go for a walk

This activity is suitable for one or two babies from 3 months up to 20 months.

What you need:

Pushchair
(double for two babies)

Yourself!

Enhancing the activity

- Go and meet your local shopkeepers.
- Plan your walks at different times of the day/week: when is the post delivered? What time does the bus service come past?
- Take a camera with you on the walk and then when you get back use the photos to make a display of the things you saw together, particularly those that really caught the babies' interest.

♪ Sing songs about what you have seen. You could try: *It's raining, it's pouring, The wheels on the bus go round and round* or *Two little dickie birds.*

This activity is a great way of communicating with babies when you are on the move outside in the fresh air. No preparation is needed and there is no cost to this activity.

What you do

1 Before you start this activity, check out your setting's relevant policies including those for Health and Safety and Outings.
2 Ideally the pushchair you use should face you and not forwards. This will ensure that you are in direct contact with babies at all times and can see them and talk to them throughout your walk.
3 Put the baby or babies in the pushchair, talking all the time about what you are doing and where you are going.
4 Depending on the weather, you may need blankets, a rain cover or sun hats and a parasol. A couple of thin blankets are better than one thick one ¬— you can take a layer away if the weather improves and they get warm.
5 Talk to them about what you are going to do 'Are you ready for a walk to the park?'
6 As you start to walk, talk to them about what you can see: 'Can you see the lovely trees…' Don't worry if they don't understand everything you say, they soon will!
7 Go on and describe what you can see: 'The trees are green and look there's a bird on a branch…" Take time to stop and look at the things you are talking about. Remember, babies need time to focus and concentrate.
8 While you talk, maintain eye contact and use facial expression and voice tone to keep them interested.
9 Talk about and show the babies different objects on your walk, and stop to look more closely at objects of interest e.g you could pick a flower or leaf to look at together.
10 Talk about what you can hear and what you can smell: 'Can you hear the birds singing?' 'Can you smell the flowers?'
11 On your walk, sing songs linked to what you have seen e.g. when passing a bus, sing *The wheels on the bus.*

TOP TIP

Go out in all weathers, and be prepared!

Look, listen and note

Does the baby…
- *Reach out to touch and grasp objects?*
- *Make sounds, coos, bubbles, babbling noises, chuckles or squeals?*
- *Smile with enjoyment?*
- *Kick and move their arms with delight?*
- *Focus on objects of interest?*

Involving parents

You could…
- *Display photographs taken on the walk to show to parents.*
- *When travelling in the car, parents could talk about things they see out of the window.*

Key words and gestures

- Use of the baby or baby's name
- Use gesture and facial expression to reinforce what you say: 'What's that?' 'What can you see?' 'Can you see the…?' 'Can you hear the…?' 'What does that feel like?' 'Well done, you are a clever boy/girl' 'What does that look like?' 'What's the weather doing?' 'It's a lovely sunny day' 'What a lovely smile' 'Are you talking to me?'
- Describe what you have seen: 'Look at the beautiful flower, it's pink.' 'What a lovely smell it has.'
- Maintain contact with the baby and use different voice tones to keep his/her attention.

Extending the challenge

- Catch a bus with one baby in the pushchair. Before your walk check with the bus company about access for pushchairs.
- For older babies:
  - Bring back items of interest seen/found – autumn is a great season to collect items such as conkers, twigs and leaves
  - Walk to the park and have a teddy bears' picnic
  - Let them walk but take the pushchair with you just in case they get tired

Mirror fun!

This activity is suitable for one baby from birth to 9 months.

What you need:

A blanket

A warm, safe place on the floor

A hand mirror

Enhancing the activity

• Use a larger mirror so you can include another baby.
• Use a favourite toy for the baby to see in the mirror.

♩ Sing any baby nursery rhymes you know or your own words to a familiar tune.

Mirrors are a very versatile resource and can be used with babies in a variety of ways. In this activity, mirrors are used as a way of communicating directly with the baby, which allows the baby to see you using the mirror.

What you do

1   Place the mat in a safe, warm place.
2   Talk to the baby as you gently put them on the blanket on their back.
3   Lie down next to the baby, as close as you can be, with your head right next to the baby's head.
4   Hold the mirror in front of both your faces, talking to the baby as you do so: 'Are you ready?' 'Here comes the mirror.' 'I can see you.'
5   Talk to the baby about anything. This could be about your day together or items of interest around the room, or you could sing a song to them.
6   Use plenty of facial expression, using your eyes, eyebrows and mouth to express yourself through sounds and words as you look at the baby in the mirror.
7   Allow time for the baby to respond to you, and imitate the sounds they make, encouraging the baby to talk back to you.
8   Move the mirror up and down, playing peek-a-boo, again using your face to communicate, as well as your voice.
9   If the baby starts to lose interest, try stroking their arms and tummy while making funny noises, blowing bubbles or just laughing with them.
10 Encourage the baby to reach out and touch the mirror, your face and body.
11 Using the mirror, observe the baby's responses. When it's time to finish the activity, pick the baby up, give them a cuddle and lots of praise.

Extending the challenge

• When the baby can reach out to grab the mirror, move the mirror slightly further away, to extend their reach.
• Place the baby on their tummy and prop the mirror in front or to the side of them (See *Tummy Time* page 16).
• Older babies who can sit unaided can sit between or in front of your legs, with the mirror in front of them, and you can play peek-a-boo.

Look, listen and note

Does the baby...
- *Raise his/her head up and down and from side to side (head control)?*
- *Respond to sounds, songs and voices?*
- *Make sounds, coos, bubbles, babbling noises or laughter?*
- *Smile with enjoyment?*

Take it outside

- Always check that babies lying on the ground are protected from the sun, from the damp and wind, from other children who may be playing nearby, and from insects or other wildlife.
- Put a blanket on a waterproof picnic blanket in a shady, safe place on the grass under a tree or bush. Take care! The sun should not shine directly on the mirror, as the reflection could damage the baby's eyes.

Involving parents

- *Take some photos and display them so parents can see how to use mirrors.*
- *Reinforce health and safety guidelines on using mirrors.*
- *Talk about the use of mirrors in the home, in the bathroom, on the dressing tables and in cars.*
- *Encourage parents to involve their children in all sorts of mirror play.*

TOP TIP
Ensure the mirrors you use are special children's mirrors (unbreakable and safe to use with babies).

Key words and gestures

- Look
- Use of the baby or babies' name
- Names of sounds
- Repeated sound and rhythmical phrases help babies language to develop
- Use gesture and facial expression to reinforce what you say: 'What a beautiful baby you are' 'Look at that lovely smile' 'I can hear you. What are you telling me?' 'That's right, what a lovely day we have had' 'What's that?' 'Look at you kicking your feet' 'I can see you' 'Well done' 'Who's a clever girl/boy?' 'Peek-a-boo' 'Look at the mirror. Is it shiny?'

Tummy time

This activity is suitable for one or two babies from birth to 9 months.

What you need:

A blanket or activity mat

A warm, safe place on the floor

A few baby toys such as rattles, soft toys, mirror and cloth books

Enhancing the activity

- Move the blanket next to a window or a mirror so the baby can see different surroundings.

- ♪ Sing a song about the toy. Make it up if you can't remember one or use a nursery rhyme or your own words to a familiar tune.

Tummy time is a key way to expand babies' physical development, especially the strength in their upper body and neck. Babies should have the opportunity for tummy time every day. You may need to persevere with some babies who may not be happy on their tummies to start with. Many babies don't spend enough time on their tummies and their development in crawling and standing may be delayed.

What you do

1 Place the mat in a safe, warm place.
2 Talk to the baby/babies as you gently put them on the blanket on their tummy. Be careful how you put them down, specially for the first few times.
3 Place toys, rattles and books around their sides and in front of their head.
4 Move the toys, creating noises to gain their interest.
5 Talk to the babies as you move each toy, encouraging them to look up at the toy.
6 If they reach out for the toy, move it into contact with their fingers and hands, praising them for effort and talking about the texture and colour.
7 Keep contact with them by stroking their back or legs.
8 If they start to lose interest, try lying down next to them so they can see you and talk to them 'You are a good boy/girl, I can see you'.
9 When tummy time is finished, carefully pick the baby up, turn them to face you and offer a cuddle and praise for doing so well on their tummy.

TOP TIP

Tummy Time is hard work and may not be as enjoyable if the baby is tired or hungry, or immediately after a feed.

Key words and gestures

- Use of the baby or babies' name
- Toy and object names
- Names of sounds
- Repeated sound and rhythmical phrases help babies language to develop
- Use gesture and facial expression to reinforce what you say: 'What's that?' 'Come on, you can do it' 'Look at you kicking your feet' 'I can see you' 'This is what you like' 'Can you see the toy?' 'Is it soft? Is it hard?' 'Well done' 'Who's a clever boy?' 'Peek-a-boo' 'Look at you holding your head up' 'Where's it gone?'

Look, listen and note

Does the baby…
- *Raise his/her head up and down and move it from side to side (head control)?*
- *Support himself/herself with extended arms?*
- *Attempt to crawl and roll?*
- *Reach out to grasp toys and objects of interest?*
- *Respond to sounds, songs and voices?*
- *Make sounds, coos, bubbles or babbling noises?*

Take it outside

- Always check to be sure babies lying on the ground are protected from the sun, from the damp and wind, from other children who may be playing nearby, and from insects or other wildlife.
- Put a blanket on a waterproof picnic blanket in a shady, safe place on the grass under a tree or bush so they can watch and listen to the leaves and the sounds as they lie on their tummies.
- Plants, trees and other children close by will provide extra interest.

Involving parents

- *Take some photos and display them, so parents can see how to do the activity.*
- *Have the activity out and show the parents how to do it.*

Extending the challenge

- Allow plenty of space around the front and back of the baby to allow for their movement.
- Sometimes carry your key babies tummy down, resting on your arms.
- For older babies who are reaching out to grab the toys, move the toys slightly further away to extend the stretching.

Mobiles

This activity is suitable for one baby from birth upwards.

What you need:

A mobile

A blanket, rug or bouncy chair

A warm safe area

Mobiles are a very popular resource and babies of all ages will enjoy them. They can be used in a variety of ways to stimulate and engage babies, encouraging them to focus and track the hanging objects. Mobiles are easy to make and can be hung in a variety of places including above cots, between furniture and outside suspended from trees.

Enhancing the activity

- Move the blanket and mobile to a different safe place – next to a window, or near a mirror.
- Place a large bright windmill near to the window but outside so the baby can gaze and watch the movement in the wind.

♪ Sing any gentle songs and lullabies such as: *Hush a bye baby, The baby in the cradle* and *This is the way we...*

What you do

1 Place the blanket in a safe, warm place.
2 Talk to the baby as you gently put them on to the blanket on their back.
3 Hang a mobile securely above the baby so they can see it. 20 to 35 cm is a good distance for babies.
4 Say 'Look, can you see? It's a ...' Remember to smile and watch for the baby's reactions.
5 Talk to the baby as you gently move the mobile.
6 If the baby reaches out for the mobile, move it into contact with their fingers and hands, praising them for effort.
7 Move the mobile gently from side to side while you sing softly to them.
8 Observe the baby's reactions and praise them when they respond through facial expression and movement of their hands and body.
9 Move the position of the mobile above the baby's legs to encourage him/her to kick the mobile with their legs and feet.
10 When the baby smiles at you, smile back and praise them.
11 When the baby has lost interest, pick them up carefully and give a loving cuddle.

Take it outside

- Always check that babies lying on the ground are protected from the sun, from the damp and wind, from other children who may be playing nearby, and from insects or other wildlife.
- Put the baby on a waterproof picnic blanket in a shady, safe place on the grass under a tree or bush so they can watch and listen to sounds of the trees moving.
- Hang objects from low branches or from a washing line or clothes airer, making sure these are securely fastened and won't blow over. Stay close all the time.

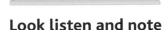

Look listen and note

Does the baby...
- *Follow your movements with his/her gaze (tracking)?*
- *Respond to sounds, songs and voices?*
- *Make sounds, bubbles or babbling noises?*
- *Reach out to touch your face, hands and fingers?*
- *Smile with enjoyment?*

Extending the challenge

- Secure a mobile between stable pieces of furniture such as chairs, but stay close to make sure they are safe. Try hanging up some everyday objects such as a wooden spoon, empty plastic water bottle or chiffon scarf. Limit the number of these objects – remember less is better for focus and attention.
- Move the position of the hanging objects so the baby can hit them with their hands, grab them or kick them with their feet. Sound-making objects (such as a rattle, keys or bunch of teaspoons) will keep them interested.
- Position the baby outside, under a full washing line.
- For older babies:
  - Use a washing line at their level with pegs and a variety of objects to be hung on the line to make their own mobiles.
  - Make a mobile of laminated photographs of the babies or their pictures.

Key words and gestures

- Look
- Use of the baby or babies' name
- Names of sounds
- Repeated sound and rhythmical phrases help babies language to develop
- Use gesture and facial expression to reinforce what you say: 'What can you see?' 'Look it's a ...' 'Can you hear the ...?' 'What a lovely noise it makes' 'Shall we sing a song?' 'Did you enjoy that?' 'That was lovely' 'I can see your beautiful smile' 'Who's a clever boy/girl?'
- Keep your face where they can see you – you need to be quite near!

Involving parents

- *You could display some suitable everyday objects to handle and hang from arches.*
- *Take some photos and display them, so parents can see how to do the activity.*

TOP TIP
Lie under the mobile yourself to see what the baby would be seeing!

Baby massage

This activity is suitable for one baby from birth to nine months.

What you need:

Baby oil – check for allergies

Changing mat, towel, blankets

A warm, safe, quiet area with minimum disruptions

Enhancing the activity

♪ Sing quiet songs.
♪ Have gentle classical music on in the background. Increase the length of massage time.
♪ Sing any gentle songs and lullabies such as: *This is the way we have a massage, Hush a bye baby, Tommy Thumb* or *This little pig.*

Massage is a form of communication and is a lovely activity for one-to-one time with a baby. It's a great way of forming attachment with your key babies, and is a very relaxing and enjoyable experience for both you and the baby.

What you do

NB: Ensure parents have given permission for this activity before you start massage sessions.

1 Ensure that you have removed any jewellery and that your hands are warm.
2 Sit on the floor and place a changing mat in front of you. Cover the changing mat with a warm soft towel and carefully place the baby on the mat.
3 Undress the baby, leaving on their nappy, telling him/her what you are doing.
4 Have a blanket nearby in case the baby gets cold.
5 Pour a little oil in to your hands and rub them together, warming the oil up saying 'Shall we have a massage?'
6 Gently begin to massage the baby's arms, legs and feet. (Search for Baby Massage on the Internet for useful websites and videos).
7 As you massage, keep eye contact with the baby and maintain verbal contact, talking to them in a quiet voice as you do so.
8 Use plenty of loving smiles and if the baby starts to cry, stop the massage and give a reassuring cuddle. Then decide whether to have a little break before you start again, or end the session for now.
9 Observe your baby and when it's time to stop, wrap the baby up in a warm towel and remove any excess oil.
10 Gently pick the baby up and give a loving cuddle. Remember they will be very relaxed and may need some quiet time after the massage.

Extending the challenge

- Progress on to the rest of the body as the baby becomes used to being massaged including back and chest.
- Introduce gentle leg and arm exercises.
- For older babies:
  - Massage the head and face. Introduce counting of toes and fingers.
  - Babies may enjoy holding a teddy or other soft toy during the massage, and they may want to give the toy a massage themselves.

Look, listen and note

Does the baby…
- *Make large movements of arms and legs?*
- *Respond to sounds, songs and voices?*
- *Make sounds, bubbles or babbling noises?*
- *Reach out to touch your face, hands and fingers?*
- *Smile with enjoyment?*
- *Fall asleep?!*

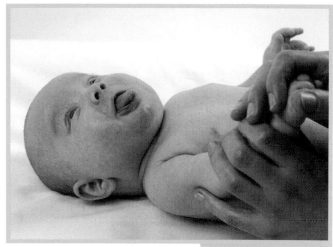

Involving parents

- *This is a perfect activity for parents to do at home with their baby, and before bedtime is an ideal time.*
- *Arrange for a baby massage training session for parents to attend.*

Key words and gestures

- Use of the baby or babies' name
- Names of sounds
- Repeated sound and rhythmical phrases help babies' language to develop
- Use gesture and facial expression to reinforce what you say: 'Do you want a massage?' 'Shall we have a massage?' 'What does that feel like?' 'That's nice' 'Can you see me?' 'Can you feel the oil on your legs/arms?' 'Did you enjoy that?' 'That was lovely' 'Who's a clever boy/girl?' 'Hush' 'Let's sing a song quietly, softly…'
- Keep your face where they can see you – you need to be quite near!

TOP TIP
Be aware of your sitting position and make sure you are comfortable.

Take it outside

- Massage is not an appropriate activity for regular use outside. However, with older babies you may find on a warm day, they may enjoy a massage lying on a blanket in the shade.

Feeding time!

This activity is suitable for one baby from 6 months up to 20 months.

What you need:

Chair for you

Highchair

Facilities to clean the baby with (water or baby wipes)

Warm and safe environment

Food and drink

Enhancing the activity

- Sit two babies side by side in highchairs to share the experience together of meal times. An extra adult may be needed to assist with the feeding of two babies.
- Explore food through senses and provide plenty of opportunities for touching the food.

- ♪ It may not always be appropriate to sing songs during meal times. However, afterwards would be a good time for a song: *Five currant buns, Jelly on a plate, Ten fat sausages* or *One potato, two potatoes.*

Using everyday events and routines is a great way to develop caring attachments with babies and children and a perfect time for this is meal times. Meal times must not be rushed and are a perfect opportunity for direct contact and communication with babies. It should be an enjoyable experience for you and for them!

What you do

1   Follow your policy and be aware of your key children's allergies and individual cultural needs. Follow your health and safety policy.
2   Carefully place a baby in to a highchair talking as you do so, 'It's dinner time, are you hungry?'
3   Sit on your chair in front of the highchair facing the baby.
4   As you feed the baby, talk to them about the food 'What are we having for lunch today? It's...'
5   Talk about the food in more detail using descriptive words, about what it tastes like, it's colour and texture, what type of food it is, and where it comes from.
6   Use plenty of voice tone and facial expression to engage them.
7   Feed the baby at their pace and don't rush the experience.
8   Praise them for enjoying the food.
9   Observe! Respond to hunger, thirst and likes and dislikes.
10 Once the baby has finished, carefully pick them up and give a reassuring cuddle while you talk to them 'Well done, you have eaten all your dinner, such a clever girl/boy!'

Take it outside

- Although meal times may be difficult to do outside, with careful planning and a little extra time, tea will be manageable outside, especially during the warmer months.
- Always check that babies are protected from the sun, from the damp and wind and from insects or other wildlife.
- Make sure highchairs are secure and on an even surface.
- Clear up any spills immediately to prevent any animals/insects being drawn to the area.

Look, listen and note

Does the baby…
- *Use body language and sounds to convey likes and dislikes?*
- *React to different textures?*
- *Jabber loudly and freely?*
- *Experiment with sounds and words?*
- *Start to feed him/herself?*

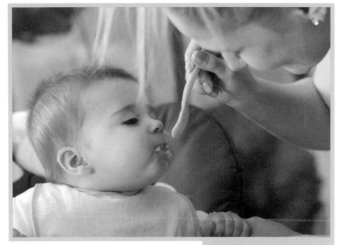

Involving parents

- *Invite parents to share food from their own cultures.*
- *Share with parents how well their babies are doing at meal times, what foods they are eating and how well they can feed themselves.*

Key words and gestures

- Use of the baby's name
- Use gesture and facial expression to reinforce what you say: 'What does that taste like?' 'Is it cold/warm etc?' 'Is it nice?' 'What a good boy you are' 'Are you hungry, thirsty?' 'What's that?' 'Are you eating…?' 'Look at the colour, it's…' 'Do you like it? It's nice.' 'It's dinner time, it's breakfast, it's tea time…' 'Mmmmm…' 'I like it too…' 'It's a vegetable/fruit…' 'What can you smell?' 'What a lovely smell, can you smell the dinner cooking?'
- Maintain contact and frequent eye contact with the baby to keep their attention.

Extending the challenge

- Let the babies feed themselves.
- Sit and eat your food with the babies.
- For older babies:
    - Sit a small group together at a low table for a very sociable experience.
    - Do a very basic cooking session together, such as making sandwiches for tea.
    - Introduce new types of foods, and foods from around the world.

TOP TIP
Enjoy the experience of feeding babies!

Goo-goo

This activity is suitable for one baby from 4 months.

What you need:

Somewhere comfortable to sit

A warm quiet area with minimum disruptions

Enhancing the activity

- Use a rattle to gain the baby's interest.
- Use daily routines, including each time you feed and change the baby, to talk to them and use these repetitive sounds.

♪ Sing songs and rhymes such as: *Row, row, row your boat, Miss Polly had a dolly* or *Wind the bobbin up*.

TOP TIP

Take your time. Allow plenty of time for the baby to respond.

This is a lovely quiet activity for a one to one session with a baby. It is the start of the baby making sounds and noises by copying you and the language you use.

What you do

1 Place the baby in to your lap facing you, making sure their head is fully supported if needed.
2 Ensure that the baby can gaze in to your face with ease and can see you (20 to 35 cm is a good distance).
3 Gain their attention by calling their name.
4 Talk to the baby using short repetitive sounds including 'goo-goo' 'mama' 'dada' 'lala' maintaining eye contact as you do so.
5 Wait for the baby to respond. If they don't respond, make the sound again.
6 Praise them for any responses they make.
7 Use plenty of facial expression with the baby to maintain interest.
8 Keep taking turns until the baby has lost interest.
9 Praise the baby while you give them a hug.

Key words and gestures

- Look
- Use of the baby or babies' name
- Names of sounds
- Repeated sound and rhythmical phrases help babies' language to develop
- Use gesture and facial expression to reinforce what you say: 'goo-goo' 'nana' 'mama' 'dada' 'lala' 'Well done, you are a clever girl/boy!' 'Can you do that?' 'I can hear you, can you hear me?' 'Can you hear the rattle?'
- Keep your face where they can see you – you need to be quite near!

Take it outside

- 'Goo-goo' is a lovely activity to do outside.
- Always check to be sure babies are protected from the sun, from the damp and wind, from other children who may be playing nearby, and from insects or other wildlife.

Look, listen and note

Does the baby...
- *Make sounds, bubbles and babbling noises?*
- *Respond to sounds, songs and voices?*
- *Follow your movements with their gaze (tracking)?*
- *Concentrate (for how long)?*
- *Begin to take turns?*
- *Smile with enjoyment?*

Involving parents

- *Use every day occurrences to talk to the baby and play the 'Goo-goo' activity – in the car, while cooking and while playing.*
- *Talk to the parents about how to do this activity at home – bring in family names and familiar home objects.*
- *Share with parents the sounds their babies are making.*

Extending the challenge

- Try passing an object, such as a soft toy or a rattle between you, as you make the sound.
- Sit with two babies next to each other, encouraging communication between you and both babies.
- For older babies:
  - Let two or more babies communicate freely between themselves with close observation.
  - Older babies love echo games. Try some simple 'My turn, your turn songs and rhymes.'
  - Use the activity to practise names of familiar objects.

Let's shake

This activity is suitable for one baby from 4 months.

What you need:

A rattle

A bouncy chair

Somewhere comfortable to sit

A warm quiet area with minimum disruptions

Enhancing the activity

- Use any objects that rattle or jingle – such as a bunch of keys.
- Introduce musical instruments including a drum or rainmaker.
- Let the baby explore the objects using their senses.
- Gently tie a small rattle or toy on to the baby's wrist, using ribbon.

♪ Sing a song about the toy. Make it up if you can't remember one or use a nursery rhyme or your own words to a familiar tune.

This activity will encourage the babies to track objects. The baby will follow the movement of objects using their gaze and listening for sounds. Little preparation is required and it is easily played in odd moments with your key babies.

What you do

1 Put the baby carefully in the bouncy chair.
2 Sit in front of the baby and ensure that the baby can gaze into your face with ease and can see you (20 to 35 cm is a good distance).
3 Gain their attention by calling their name.
4 Gently shake the rattle, saying, 'Can you hear the rattle?'
5 Wait for the baby to respond.
6 Bring the rattle to the baby to allow them to touch and explore.
7 Praise them for any responses they make.
8 Move the rattle gently away from the baby and shake it carefully: at the side of the baby, behind the baby, above the baby or hide the rattle in your hands as you shake it.
9 Observe the baby's reactions – have they followed the movement and sound of the rattle?
10 Remember to use plenty of praise and facial expressions.
11 Keep going until the baby loses interest.

Extending the challenge

- Shake the rattle differently – quietly and loudly.
- Focus on just movement of an object by replacing a rattle with a soft toy.
- Find or buy some wrist or ankle bells for babies, so they can make the sounds for themselves.
- For older babies:
  - Shake the rattle just once!
  - Make some simple home made rattles from empty containers.
  - Play peek-a-boo
  (see *Peek-a-boo* page 8)

Look, listen and note

Does the baby…
- *Follows movements with their gaze (tracking)?*
- *Makes sounds, bubbles or babbling noises?*
- *Respond to sounds, songs and voices*
- *Reach out to grab the rattle?*
- *Concentrate (for how long)?*
- *Smile and kick with enjoyment?*

Take it outside

- Always check to be sure babies are protected from the sun, from the damp and wind, from other children who may be playing nearby and from insects or other wildlife.
- Use the outdoor objects – follow the movement of trees, leaves and wildlife. Listen out for sounds and share them with the baby: 'Can you hear the birds singing?'

TOP TIP
Take your time! Allow plenty of time for the baby to respond.

Involving parents

- *Demonstrate to parents how to do this activity.*
- *Talk to the parents about doing this activity at home – they could bring in familiar home objects to track and listen to.*

Key words and gestures

- Use of the baby or babies' name
- Names of sounds
- Repeated sound and rhythmical phrases help babies' language to develop
- Use gesture and facial expression to reinforce what you say: 'Can you hear the rattle?' 'Where has the rattle gone?' 'Is it behind you/at the side of you?' 'What noise does that make?' 'Is it loud or soft?' 'What a clever boy/girl you are!' 'Can you see the rattle?'
- Keep your face where they can see you – you need to be quite near!

Where are those toes?

This activity is suitable for one baby from 5 months.

What you need:

A blanket

Enhancing the activity

- Use a piece of fabric or a feather to tickle between the baby's feet and toes.
- Allow time for babies to explore their toes during nappy time.
- Lay the baby in front of you and let them look at the movement of your feet and toes. Make sure your feet are clean!

♩ Sing a song about toes – make it up if you can't remember one – or use a nursery rhyme or your own words to a familiar tune: *This little piggy, Round and round the garden, Put your toes in the air* or *Head, shoulders, knees and toes*

TOP TIP

Be aware of baby's likes and dislikes. Not all babies will enjoy their feet being played with.

No resources are necessary except a baby! This is an instant activity with no preparation, which you can do absolutely anywhere. Once a baby has found their toes, they are fascinated with them and just want to explore them at every opportunity! Babies should spend part of every day with bare feet, so they can experience finding their feet and toes, and experiencing objects and surfaces with their feet.

What you do

1 Sit on the floor, with the baby in your lap, facing sideways. Support them if needed.
2 Take off the baby's socks, talking to them about what you are doing: 'Lets take your socks off – pop goes a sock! And pop goes the other one!'
3 Gently hold the baby's toes, saying, 'Where are your toes?'
4 Softly move the legs and feet up and down.
5 Wait for the baby to respond.
6 Laugh and use plenty of facial expression as you tickle their feet.
7 Give a reassuring cuddle.
8 Lift the baby up and carefully place them on the blanket in front of you.
9 Gently blow on their toes. After a few times, blow raspberries on their toes.
10 Hold the baby's feet and play peek-a-boo between them.
11 Allow time for the baby to reach and grab their legs, feet and toes.

Take it outside

- This is a lovely activity to play outside on a blanket on a warm day.
- Always check to be sure babies are protected from the sun, from the damp and wind, from other children who may be playing nearby and from insects or other wildlife.
- Use outdoor objects such as grass and leaves to tickle their feet.

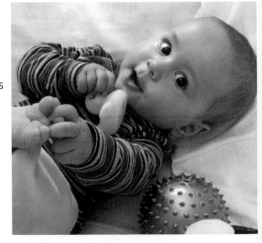

Look, listen and note

Does the baby…
- *Reach out to grab their feet and toes?*
- *Smile and kick with enjoyment?*
- *Make sounds, bubbles or babbling noises?*
- *Respond to sounds, songs and voices?*
- *Use physical movement (roll on to their side)?*
- *Put their toes in their own mouth?*

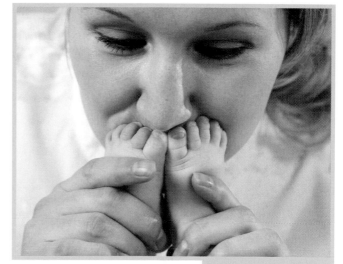

Key words and gestures

- Use of the baby or babies' name
- Names of sounds
- Repeated sound and rhythmical phrases help babies' language to develop
- Use gesture and facial expression to reinforce what you say: 'Where are those toes?' 'Are they hiding beneath your socks?' 'I can see your toes' 'Let's tickle them' 'Did you like that?' 'Peek-a-boo' 'How many toes have you got?' 'Let's count, one…' 'Your toes are so soft' 'Can you see my toes?' 'What a clever boy/girl you are!'
- Keep your face where they can see you – you need to be quite near!

Involving parents

- *Talk to the parents about doing this activity at home – exploring feet during nappy changing and bath time.*
- *Explain the importance of letting their babies go barefoot for some of every day throughout childhood. Socks can be very restraining, and babies don't need shoes!*

Extending the challenge

- Play peek-a-boo with the baby's toes by hiding them behind their socks.
- Provide opportunities for the baby to have no socks on during the day to encourage playing with toes when they choose too!
- For older babies:
  - Ensure there is enough space for the baby to roll about playing with their toes.
  - Count the toes.
  - Make sock puppets.

Baby echo

This activity is suitable for one baby from four months.

What you need:

One baby

Somewhere comfortable to sit

A warm, safe, quiet area with minimum disruptions

Enhancing the activity

- By adding other resources, taking it somewhere else or working with more children
- Use a rattle or a toy to gain the baby's interest.
- Use daily routines, including each time you feed and change the baby, to talk to them and use repetitive sounds and expressions.

♪ Use songs and rhymes such as: *I Spy with my little eye, I hear with my little ears, Little Peter Rabbit* or *Heads, shoulders, knees and toes.*

This is a lovely quiet time activity for one-to-one time with a baby. It is the start of the baby making sounds and noises by copying you and the expressions and simple sounds you use and make.

What you do

1 Place the baby in to your lap facing you, making sure their head fully supported if needed. Put them on a cushion in your lap if that is more comfortable.
2 Ensure that the baby can gaze in to your face with ease and can see you. 20 to 35 cm is a good distance.
3 Gain their attention by calling their name.
4 Use exaggerated expressions and a lively voice to maintain their interest.
5 Use a variety of facial expressions and sounds encouraging the baby to watch and copy you:
   - open your mouth wide
   - raise your eye brows
   - make a kiss with your lips
   - blow out your cheeks
   - blink your eyes
6 Allow time for the baby to respond and copy you.
7 Praise the baby while you give them a hug.

TOP TIP

Even newborn babies will respond to exaggerated and slow facial expressions.

Look, listen and note

Does the baby…
- *Make sounds, bubbles or babbling noises?*
- *Copy your expressions and sounds?*
- *Respond to sounds, songs and voices?*
- *Follow your movements with their gaze (tracking)*
- *Concentrate? How long before they respond?*

Involving parents

- *Show parents how to do this activity.*
- *Suggest they use every day occurrences to talk to the baby and use expressions – during nappy changing and while playing.*
- *Share with parents the sounds and expressions their babies are making.*

Key words and gestures

- Use of the baby's name
- Names of sounds
- Repeated sound and rhythmical phrases help babies language to develop.
- Use gesture and facial expression to reinforce what you say: 'Goo-goo' 'Nana' 'Mama' 'Dada' 'Lala' 'Well done you are a clever girl/boy!' 'Can you do that?' 'Where are my eyes, ears…?' 'Here is my tongue.' 'Look at your…'
- Keep your face where they can see you – you need to be quite near!

Extending the challenge

- Use a mirror so the baby can see themselves and you making expressions.
- For older babies:
  - Let two or more babies communicate freely between themselves with close observation.
  - Show more complicated expressions to copy.
  - Encourage them to respond with sounds and respond to them with words.

Take it outside

- 'Baby echo' is a lovely activity outside.
- Always check to be sure babies are protected from the sun, from the damp and wind, from other children who may be playing nearby, and from insects or other wildlife.
- Play the game while the baby is in a pushchair during a walk.

Smiling faces

This activity is suitable for one baby from birth to 6 months.

What you need:

A card circle or small paper plate

A black felt pen, a chopstick or wooden spoon, glue or tape

Comfortable chair for you

A warm, safe quiet area

Involving parents

- *Take some photos and display them, so parents can see how you do the activity.*
- *Demonstrate the activity.*
- *Make a booklet of rhymes and songs for parents to use at home.*

This is a lovely activity for quiet time with your key babies. It will give you quality uninterrupted time with the baby when you can form and develop good attachment while encouraging the baby to copy your facial expressions. It can easily be adapted for older babies and for more than one baby.

What you do

1 Make a face puppet by drawing a very simple smiling face in black felt pen on the paper plate or card circle. Attach the face to a stick or wooden spoon.
2 Place the baby in your lap, or securely propped on a cushion facing you, making sure their head is fully supported if needed.
3 Ensure that the baby can gaze in to your face with ease (20 to 35 cm is a good distance).
4 Sing 'Hello' to the baby. Stroke the baby's cheeks and gently engage his/her attention.
5 Now move the face puppet into the baby's field of vision, saying 'Who is this?'
6 Gently and very slowly move the puppet from side to side. Make sure you do this slowly, so the baby can track the face as it passes in front of his/her.
7 Allow plenty of time for the baby to respond and react to the face, and talk gently and reassuringly as you work together.
8 Use lots of praise as the baby follows the face and perhaps smiles back at it.
9 Keep talking and playing while the baby is happy and involved. Don't go on too long!

Take it outside

- Sit outside, under a tree in the shade and play with the puppets together.
- Hang smiling faces from bushes and low branches, or from a frame or washing line.
- Always check to be sure babies lying on the ground are protected from the sun, from the damp and wind, from other children who may be playing nearby, and from insects and other wildlife.

Look, listen and note

Does the baby…
- *Make sounds, bubbles or babbling noises?*
- *Follow the puppet, moving their eyes or turning their head?*
- *Respond by smiling at the face?*
- *Follow your movements with their gaze (tracking)?*
- *Show head control?*
- *Concentrate? How long before they respond?*
- *Enjoy the activity with smiles and laughter?*

Enhancing the activity

- Make some other black and white patterns on plates or circles, and use these in the same way. Black and white patterns will help the baby to focus.
- Make a simple black and white mobile of faces to hang above the changing table.

♪ Sing a song about faces. Make it up if you can't remember one or use a nursery rhyme or your own words to a familiar tune, such as:
Twinkle, twinkle little star:
Can you see my smiling face?
Move it to another place,
I can see it over here,
Now it's moving over there,
Can you see my smiling face?
Move it to another place.

Key words and gestures

- Use of the baby's name
- Face
- Names of sounds
- Repeated sound and rhythmical phrases help babies' language to develop
- Remember to move the puppet very slowly, taking cues from the baby as they track the movement.
- Use comforting words and such phrases as: 'What's that?' 'Can you see the face?' 'What a lovely smile' 'Can you see it over here?'
- Keep the face where they can see it, but not too close! Watch their eyes for clues.

Extending the challenge

- Try sticking a small unbreakable mirror on a stick and holding this where the baby can see her/his reflection. S/he won't recognise her/himself but will respond.
- For older babies:
  - Let 'sitting babies' play with the paper face plates, but supervise carefully if they have sticks!
  - Stick photos of other children or adults in the setting on paper plates for more games.

TOP TIP
Allow plenty of time for the baby to respond.

Musical instruments

This activity is suitable for one or two babies from 6 months.

What you need:

A selection of musical instruments

A blanket

A large basket

A warm, safe area to play the instruments – be aware that the activity may become noisy

Enhancing the activity

• Encourage turn taking

♪ Use musical instruments during a singing session

This is a lively activity and provides the opportunity for babies to hear different sounds while copying, taking turns and enjoying the experience of music.

What you do

1 Place the two babies on the blanket, facing each other, while you sit next to them. Have the container of musical instruments beside you.
2 Shake an instrument to gain the babies' attention and interest saying, 'Listen, what can you hear?' Observe the babies. Did they both follow the sound?
3 Bring the container out and place it on the floor between the babies, saying 'Look what we can play with – some musical instruments.'
4 Allow time for the babies to explore the musical instruments by themselves.
5 Pick up a musical instrument, one at a time, and shake it, making a noise and telling the babies the name of the instrument.
6 Give each baby a musical instrument and let them experiment with the instrument and the sounds it makes. You have one too.
7 Encourage the babies to listen to the sounds of the musical instruments and to take turns in making sounds.
8 Once the babies begin to lose interest, swap the musical instruments and give them another one to explore.
9 Keep talking and playing the musical instruments while the babies are happy and involved. Don't go on too long!

Extending the challenge

• Sort musical instruments and introduce one type at a time.
• Play the musical instruments quickly, slowly, quietly or loudly.
• Older babies could:
  • Make their own musical instruments.
  • Play recognition games with musical instruments.
  • Copy you as you shake a simple rhythm.
  • Play starting and stopping games with musical instruments.
  • Sing a song about music, such as: *I am the music man, I can play on the big bass drum, This old man* or *If you're happy and you know it*

Look, listen and note

Does the baby…
- *Make sounds, bubbles or babbling noises?*
- *Copy adults or other babies?*
- *Respond to sounds, songs and voices?*
- *Begin to co-ordinate hands to play simple musical instruments?*
- *Follow the movements with his/her gaze (tracking)?*
- *Concentrate. How long until he/she responds?*
- *Enjoy the activity?*

Key words and gestures

- Use of the baby's name
- Toy and object names
- Names of sounds
- Repeated sound and rhythmical phrases help babies' language to develop
- Use gesture and facial expression to reinforce what you say: 'What's that?' 'Can you copy me?' 'Listen' 'Let's do this together' 'What sounds does that make?' 'Is it noisy, quiet, quick or slow?' 'What instrument have you got? It's a…' 'Look it's a wooden instrument' 'What does that feel like?' 'Well done, what a clever boy/girl!'
- Keep your face where they can see you – you need to be quite close!

Take it outside

- A lovely activity to do outside, as you can make as much noise as you like!
- Always check to be sure babies lying or sitting on the ground are protected from the sun, from the damp and wind, from other children who may be playing nearby, and from insects and other wildlife.

Involving parents

- *Take some photos and display them, so parents can see how you do the activity and how much fun musical instruments are.*
- *Demonstrate the activity and show the parents how to improvise at home with simple objects such as saucepans and spoons.*
- *Make a booklet of rhymes and songs for parents to use at home.*

TOP TIP
Be aware babies need time to get used to holding musical instruments carefully, so supervise closely.

Pop goes the bubble!

This activity is suitable for one or two babies from 3 months upwards.

What you need:

Bubbles (you can buy these in bulk from educational suppliers)

An adult

Enhancing the activity

- Use a variety of different types of wands including different sizes and shapes.
- Get a bubble machine.

♪ Sing a song. Make it up if you can't remember one or use a nursery rhyme or your own words to a familiar tune, such as: *Pat a Cake*

Bubbles are inexpensive, magical and captivating for adults and babies, so this is a very enjoyable activity for both. Bubbles are also a great way of gaining children's attention, so learn to use this very simple attention grabber!

What you do

1 Place the baby in an upright position. This could be in a bouncy chair or sitting with another adult. Older babies will be able to sit unaided.
2 Sit in front of them and ensure you are at their level, where they can see you.
3 Gently blow the bubbles around the babies avoiding their faces, and specially their eyes.
4 As you blow the bubbles talk to the babies about what you are doing: 'Let's blow some bubbles!'
5 To maintain their interest, blow the bubbles near them, where they can see and reach out for them. Try blowing bubbles around their hands and feet so they can touch the bubbles.
6 Try to blow the bubbles slowly, catch a bubble on the wand and move it to where the babies can see it and can pop the bubble.
7 Use different blowing techniques to make small or large bubbles, single or groups of bubbles.
8 Use plenty of facial expression and maintain close contact throughout the activity
9 Stop the activity as soon as they lose interest.

Extending the challenge

- Play popping and patting games with the bubbles. Use a variety of different surfaces to provide different textures for the baby or babies to experience when popping the bubbles. This could include crinkly materials and soft fabrics.
- For older babies:
  - Sit with a baby at the water tray full of lots of bubbles.
  - Wash clothes and dolls in the water tray with extra bubbles.

Look, listen and note

Does the baby…
- *Follow the movement of bubbles (tracking)?*
- *Show facial expression of delight and enjoyment?*
- *Respond to a familiar adult?*
- *Make sounds, coos, bubbles, babbling noises, chuckling or squeals?*
- *Reach out and try to grasp and pop the bubbles using fingers and hands?*
- *Move his/her arms and legs?*
- *Show head control?*

Key words and gestures

- Use of the baby or babies' name
- Use gesture and facial expression to reinforce what you say: 'Let's blow bubbles' 'What's that?' 'Where have the bubbles gone?' 'Oh no, the bubbles have popped!' 'What a clever girl/boy you are.' 'One, two, three…' 'Look how beautiful the bubbles are.' 'Well done.' 'What a beautiful smile you have.' 'What a big bubble' 'It's round' 'Look at the lovely colours'
- Maintain contact with the babies and use different voice tones to keep their attention

Involving parents

- *Washing up at the sink and bath time are excellent opportunities to blow bubbles with your babies at home.*
- *Take photographs of the babies' expressions of delight during watching and popping the bubbles. Share these with parents.*

Take it outside

- This activity is perfect for outdoor play.
- If you take bouncy chairs outside, ensure they are positioned on level ground and are safe before putting the baby in to the chair.
- Use the weather to extend the activity – sunshine to enhance the colours of the bubbles and the wind to move the bubbles around.
- Larger wands are perfect for using outside.

TOP TIP
Remember to avoid getting bubbles in babies' faces, especially their eyes.

Drip, drop!

This activity is suitable for one baby from 6 months.

What you need:

Washing up bowl or container

Towels

Clothes for any spills – these must be wiped up immediately

A warm, safe room with a non slip vinyl floor

Enhancing the activity

- Use a variety of water toys or containers.
- Paddle in the water.
- Use the sink.

♪ Sing a song about the game. Make it up if you can't remember one or use a nursery rhyme or your own words to a familiar tune such as: *I hear thunder, Row row your boat* or *The big ship sails*.

TOP TIP
Be careful that the baby does not pull the bowl over!

Water play is a popular sensory activity, and can be very soothing for babies. Minimum resources are needed for such an exciting experience where you can introduce textures, sounds and lots of fun and enjoyment. All ages enjoy water!

What you do

1 Half fill the washing up bowl with warm water and place on a towel on the floor.
2 Sit on the floor next to the bowl with the baby sitting on your lap, facing sideways. Have an extra towel next to you.
3 Introduce the water to the baby by gently splashing the water with your fingers: 'Look what we have here – it's some water.'
4 Maintain eye contact with the baby as you do so and offer a reassuring hug if needed.
5 Hold the baby securely and allow their fingers to touch the water, talking as you do so: 'Do you want to feel the water?'
6 Offer lots of praise as the baby plays with the water.
7 Gently splash the baby and wait to see if they copy and what their reaction is.
8 Keep talking and playing while the baby is happy and involved.

Key words and gestures

- Use of the baby's name
- Toy and object names
- Names of sounds
- Repeated sound and rhythmical phrases help babies' language to develop.
- Use gesture and facial expression to reinforce what you say: 'Look there is some water?' 'What does that feel like?' 'Is it hot, cold, wet...' 'Can you splash?' 'Don't splash me!' 'What's that?' 'Can you copy me?' 'Let's do this together' 'Let's make some bubbles' 'Pour, drop, drip, full, empty...' 'Here it comes' 'Are you ready?' 'Splash down'
- Keep your face where they can see you – you need to be quite close!

Look, listen and note

Does the baby…
* *Make sounds, bubbles or babbling noises?*
* *Copy your actions or words?*
* *Reach and grab?*
* *Respond to sounds, songs and voices?*
* *Follow movements with their gaze (tracking)?*
* *Concentrate? How long before they respond?*
* *Enjoy the activity with smiles and laughter?*

Take it outside

* A lovely activity to do outside sitting under a tree in the shade.
* Always check that babies lying on the ground are protected from the sun, from the damp and wind, from other children who may be playing nearby, and from insects and other wildlife.
* Use a paddling pool but remember to follow your health and safety procedures.

Involving parents

* *Take photographs of the babies' expressions of delight during water play and share these with parents.*
* *This is a perfect activity to do at home in the sink or in the bath.*
* *Provide information on local baby and toddler swimming sessions.*

Extending the challenge

* Use the water tray and have two babies playing. You will need another adult to help you.
* Try warmer and cooler water.
* For older babies:
  * Colour the water
  * Add bubbles
  * Go outside in the rain with Wellington boots, waterproofs and umbrellas.

Feely box

This activity is suitable for one baby from 6 months.

What you need:

An empty shoebox or container with a lid

Shredded paper

A variety of objects: a spoon, a sponge, or a favourite toy

A blanket

A warm, safe area

Enhancing the activity

- Explore the shredded paper with feet.
- Use different materials in the box, such as sand or fabric.

♪ Sing a song about the game. Make it up if you can't remember one or use a nursery rhyme or your own words to a familiar tune such as: *Here is a box, Can you find it? (to the tune of I hear thunder)* or *We can play on the big, big box*

This is a lovely sensory activity, which introduces new textures and materials to young babies, and can be easily adapted to the resources available in your setting. With a bit of imagination, who needs expensive toys and equipment?

What you do

1 Put the shredded paper in the shoe box and put the lid on.
2 Place the blanket in a warm safe area.
3 Sit on the blanket with the baby facing you.
4 Bring the shoebox into view talking 'Look! What have we got here?'
5 Tap on the shoebox to gain the baby's attention.
6 Allow time for the baby to copy and explore the outside of the box.
7 Carefully open the box talking with expressive language: 'What's in here?'
8 Allow the baby to explore the shredded paper using their hands and fingers.
9 Keep talking and investigating the box while the baby is happy and involved.
10 Introduce an object such as a spoon. Place the spoon in the box, hidden by the shredded paper: 'Where's the spoon? Can you find it?'
11 Let the baby explore and find the spoon, offering praise with their response. Help them if needed.
12 Once the baby has lost interest, put the shredded paper back in the box, close the lid and finish the activity with a hug and lots of praise.

Extending the challenge

- Have more than one baby, and make two feely boxes.
- Sit together at a table and explore textures.
- For older babies:
  - Let them sit unaided without your support
  - Instead of a shoebox use a builder's tray. More than one baby can explore in this larger area.
  - Use smaller objects for the babies to find.
  - Turn the feely box into the 'seaside', using sand with shells and pebbles.

Look, listen and note

Does the baby...
- *Make sounds, bubbles or babbling noises?*
- *Copy movements and explore?*
- *Respond to sounds, songs and voices?*
- *Follow the movements with their gaze (tracking)*
- *Show hand and eye coordination?*
- *Concentrate? How long before they respond?*
- *Smile and laugh to show enjoyment?*

TOP TIP

Remember how much the baby has enjoyed the experience – don't worry about the mess!

Key words and gestures

- Use of the baby's name
- Toy and object names
- Names of sounds
- Repeated sound and rhythmical phrases help babies' language to develop
- Use gesture and facial expression to reinforce what you say: 'What's that?' 'What's in the box?' 'Is it a drum?' 'Let's make some noise' 'Loud, quiet' 'Let's do this together' 'What does that feel like?' 'Is it soft, hard, rough, smooth...?' 'Look. It's shredded paper...' 'Shall we hide the...?' 'Where's the... is it hidden?' 'Well done, what a clever boy/girl!' 'Let's close the box'
- Keep your face where they can see you – you need to be quite close!

Involving parents

- *Take some photos and display them, so parents can see how you do the activity and how their baby enjoys exploring.*
- *Show the parents how to do the activity at home – they could use a washing up bowl or a bucket instead of a shoebox.*

Take it outside

- If it's windy, the shredded paper may blow everywhere! So this is an activity to do on a still day.
- Always check that babies lying or sitting on the ground are protected from the sun, from the damp and wind, from other children who may be playing nearby, and from insects and other wildlife.

Activity mat

This activity is suitable for one or two babies from birth to 9 months.

What you need:

An activity mat or a small blanket or piece of soft material

A warm, safe place on the floor

A few baby toys such as rattles, soft baby toys

Enhancing the activity

- Move the mat to a different safe place – next to a window, near a mirror, or where the baby can see other children playing.

Activity mats are popular and useful resources. Working with familiar resources helps to develop early language skills. Of course babies will sometimes play on activity mats without adult support, although you should always be close at hand. This activity will help babies to get the most out of a familiar situation.

What you do

1. Place the mat in a safe, warm place.
2. Talk to the baby or babies as you gently put them on the mat (on their backs to start with).
3. Choose a toy and bring it near the babies so they can see it. (20 to 35 cm is a good distance.)
4. Say 'Look, look, it's a ...' Remember to smile and watch for the babies' reactions.
5. Talk to the baby or babies as you move the toy gently to keep their attention by movement, sound or the colour and shape of the toy.
6. If a baby reaches out for the toy, move it into contact with their fingers and hands, praising them for effort and talking about the texture and colour of the toy.
7. Now choose a different toy (changing the type, or sound it makes).
8. Follow the same process of talking, moving the toy and praising the baby's response.
9. Keep playing, talking and changing the toys while the babies are happy and involved. Don't go on too long!

Key words and gestures

- Use of the baby or babies' name
- Toy and object names
- Names of sounds
- Repeated sound and rhythmical phrases help babies' language to develop
- Use gesture and facial expression to reinforce what you say: 'What's that?' 'This one?' 'This is what you like.' 'Who's a clever boy/girl!' 'Where's it gone?'
- Keep your face where they can see you – you need to be quite near!

Look, listen and note

Does the baby…
* *Focus on objects, and respond to different toys? (name these)*
* *Follow moving objects with their gaze (tracking)?*
* *Respond to sounds, songs, and voices?*
* *Makes sounds, bubbles or babbling noises?*
* *Grasp, kick, reach and show growing control of this?*
* *Stay engaged (for how long)?*

Take it outside

* Always check that babies lying on the ground are protected from the sun, from the damp and wind, from other children who may be playing nearby, and from insects or other wildlife.
* Put the activity mat on a waterproof picnic blanket in a shady, safe place on the grass under a tree or bush so they can watch and listen to the leaves and the sounds.
* Hang objects from low branches or from a washing line or clothes airer make sure these are securely fastened and won't blow over. Stay close all the time.

Extending the challenge

* Add one or two arches, so you can hang a single toy to talk about together. If you haven't got arches, you could use a baby mobile on a stable piece of furniture such as a chair, but stay with them to make sure they are safe.
* Try some everyday objects such as a wooden spoon, empty plastic water bottle or chiffon scarf. Limit the number of objects, remember less is better when babies are practising focusing.
* Move the position of the hanging objects so the baby can hit them with their hands or grab them. Sound-making objects (such as a rattle, keys or bunch of teaspoons) will keep them interested.
* Put the babies on their tummies (see Tummy Time page*).
* For older babies:
  * Position the hanging objects above the baby's legs and feet and allow them to kick .
  * Sing a song about the toy you are using. Make it up if you can't remember one or use a nursery rhyme or your own words to a familiar tune.

Involving parents

* Take some photos and display them, so parents can see how you do the activity.
* Have the activity out and show the parents how to do it.
* Talk to parents about using everyday materials and objects for this activity.
* Display some suitable everyday objects to handle and hang from arches.

TOP TIP
This activity doesn't need expensive resources – the baby, you, a rug, and a quiet corner with an everyday object can be just as successful in encouraging communication.

My first paddle

This activity is suitable for one baby from 5 months.

What you need:

A warm sunny day

A small baby's paddling pool, baby bath or large washing up bowl

Warm water

A warm, safe, shady area outside

Enhancing the activity

- Put some bath ducks or other water toys in the paddling pool.
- Add some bubbles but be aware of sensitive skin conditions

♪ Sing a song – make it up if you can't remember one – or use a nursery rhyme or your own words to a familiar tune: *Row, row, row your boat, The big ship sails, Five little ducks* or *Rub a dub dub.*

On a warm sunny day, a paddle in a paddling pool is a perfect way of keeping a baby's body temperature at a safe level. Babies will enjoy kicking and splashing their toes in the water, and what a lovely way to introduce a sensory communication activity!

What you do

1 Check and follow your Health and Safety policy before you start this activity.
2 In a warm but shady area outside, put some warm water in the paddling pool. You will not need much water – a couple of inches is plenty.
3 Place some towels next to the paddling pool.
4 Take the baby outside, talking about what you are about to do 'Shall we go for a paddle?'.
5 Take off the baby's socks and roll up their trousers if necessary.
6 Hold the baby safely, ensuring their head is supported.
7 Gently lower the baby so just their toes are in the water. Lift their toes in and out of the water a couple of times, getting the baby used to the temperature and experience.
8 Allow time for the baby to respond.
9 When the baby is familiar with the water, carefully start to make splashes with the baby's toes laughing and talking as you do so.
10 Maintain contact with the baby and observe the baby's reactions. Stop when the baby has lost interest, or if they become distressed.
11 Give the baby a hug while you dry their toes.

Extending the challenge

- With support from another adult, have two babies paddling together.
- For older babies:
  - Put on their swimwear and nappies to fully paddle in the water.
  - Use different types of water toys or just boats.
  - Be very careful about slipping on wet surfaces or the bottom of pools.

Look, listen and note

Does the baby…
- *Make sound, bubbles or babbling noises?*
- *Respond to sounds, songs and voices*
- *Track?*
- *Kick and splash?*
- *Express fun and enjoyment with smiles and laughter?*

Key words and gestures

- Use of the baby's name
- Names of sounds
- Repeated sound and rhythmical phrases help babie's language to develop
- Use gesture and facial expression to reinforce what you say: 'Shall we go for a paddle?' 'Are you ready?' 'Let's go for a paddle' 'Ready, three, two, one splash down!' 'Can you splash with your toes?' 'Is it cold, warm…?' 'What can you hear?' 'Splash!' 'You can do it, let's kick those toes!' 'What's that?' 'I can hear your… can you?' 'Well done, what a clever boy/girl!' 'Listen' 'It sounds like…' 'That was lovely'
- Keep your face where they can see you.

Involving parents

- Take some photos and display them, so parents can see how you do the activity and how much fun it can be.
- How to adapt this activity using the bath or sink at home.
- Remind parents about the safety of this activity, and the importance of never leaving babies or small children alone near water, even if it is a shallow pool.

Take it inside

- Indoors this is an 'any time of the year' activity!
- Use a washing up bowl or large container on a non-slip floor and have plenty of old towels handy, so you can mop up spills immediately.

TOP TIP
Remember the dangers of water. Never leave a baby on their own near water!

Way up high!

This activity is suitable for one baby from 4 months up to 20 months.

What you need:

A safe environment with enough room to turn around in

Yourself!

Enhancing the activity

- Instead of aeroplanes, be 'helicopters' 'rockets' or 'birds'
- Don't strain your back. With older babies, play aeroplanes at your waist level and not above your head as babies get heavier and more wriggly.
- Use picture books to talk about what an aeroplane is.

♪ Sing a song. Make it up if you can't remember one or use a nursery rhyme or your own words to a familiar tune such as: *See the little aeroplanes, aeroplanes* or *aeroplanes all in a row*.

This fun simple activity will help babies to become active. No resources are needed apart from yourself and the baby so you can play aeroplanes anywhere and at anytime, and babies love it! NB: The baby must have head control.

What you do

1 Talk to the baby about what you are going to do, 'Shall we be aeroplanes? Let's start to fly!'
2 Holding the baby facing you, start to lift the baby up above your head.
3 Once your arms are fully stretched, gently move the baby from side to side, then round and round.
4 Blow on the baby's face gently, laughing as you do so.
5 Constantly keep eye contact with the baby and use a variety of voice tones and facial expressions while talking and playing aeroplanes.
6 Slowly bring the baby back down to your level giving a cuddle as you do so and talking about what they have just done 'You have been flying, did you enjoy that?'
7 If the baby is still interested and happy, repeat the activity.
8 Observe the baby's responses and stop once interest has been lost. Don't continue if they are at all distressed.

Take it outside

- 'Aeroplanes' is easily transferred to outside and the freedom of outdoor play will enhance the activity by large movements from yourself. Make sure you are standing on a level surface!
- Show real aeroplanes in the sky and listen to the noises they make.

Extending the challenge

- As the baby becomes more confident with aeroplanes, start to move the baby up and down more quickly, rotate round and round and move around the room.
- For older babies:
  - Talk about holidays – have they been on an aeroplane?
  - Look at different types of transport.

TOP TIP
Straight after meal times is NOT a good time to do this activity!

Look, listen and note

Does the baby…
- *Make sounds, cooing noises, bubbles, babbling or gurgling noises, chuckling or squeals?*
- *Show a delighted response to the active play?*
- *Smile with enjoyment?*
- *Interact and engage with a familiar adult?*
- *Move and kick legs and arms?*
- *Show head control is improving?*
- *Focus and maintain eye contact?*
- *Stay engaged (for how long)?*

Involving parents

- *Demonstrate to parents this simple activity and how babies enjoy this one-to-one time with an adult.*
- *Share songs and rhymes with parents to sing while playing 'aeroplanes'. You could give them a song sheet to take home.*
- *Ask parents about any forthcoming holidays.*
- *Dads love this activity too, but you may need to remind them to be gentle!*

Key words and gestures

- Use of the baby's name
- Use gesture and facial expression to reinforce what you say: 'Let's go flying?' 'What's that?' 'How's that?' 'Ready, steady, go.' 'One, two, three…' 'Look at you, you're flying!' 'Where are we going?' 'Did you enjoy flying?' 'Up and down, round and round.' 'Well done, you are a clever boy/girl!' 'What does that feel like?' 'NYAAOW.' 'BRRRRR…'
- Maintain eye contact with the baby and use different voice tones to focus their attention.

All fall down!

This activity is suitable for one or two babies from 4 to 9 months.

What you need:

Stacking beakers

A wall mirror or children's hand mirror

A few soft baby toys

A soft blanket

A warm, safe place on the floor

Enhancing the activity

- Put a soft baby toy at the top of the tower.
- Play with two babies and build a tower for each of them.
- Place the baby or babies on to their backs and build the tower next to them, ensuring the tower is in reach of their fingers, encouraging them to turn their head and perhaps even roll over onto their side.

♪ Sing a song – make it up if you can't remember one – or use a nursery rhyme or your own words to a familiar tune: *Humpty Dumpty, London Bridge is falling down* or *Ten green bottles*

Stacking beakers are a very versatile, and can be a cheap resource. Babies from an early age will respond to the colour and size of the beakers and this activity can be adapted for older children. Use plenty of talk to accompany the actions and sounds.

What you do

1 Place the soft blanket on to the floor in a safe, warm place.
2 Sit on the blanket, in front of the mirror, supporting a younger baby between your legs. Older babies will be able to sit unaided.
3 Start to build a tower in front of the babies. (16 to 20 cm is a good distance for babies to see.)
4 As you build the tower talk to them about what you are doing: 'Let's build a tower'
5 To maintain interest, draw attention to each beaker by gently tap down as you make sounds and exaggerate the movement in front of the babies line of vision.
6 Once you have built the tower, knock it down to show them what happens. As you knock the tower over, talk to them about what you are doing, and anticipating the collapse 'The tower is going to fall down…' Use plenty of voice tone as you do this and give a reassuring cuddle in delight as the tower falls.
7 If the babies reach out for the tower, let them make contact with their fingers and hands, praising them for effort and talking about the tower falling down. Let them hold a beaker.
8 Use the mirror in front of you to observe their responses and to allow them to see your facial expression as you build and rebuild the tower.
9 Follow the same process of building and knocking the tower over talking and interacting throughout.
10 Keep praising and talking, maintaining their interest with the beakers.

Take it outside

- Always check that babies lying on the ground are protected from the sun, from the damp and wind, from other children who may be playing nearby, and from insects or other wildlife.
- Use a waterproof picnic blanket in a shady, safe place on the grass and follow the activity as described above.
- If you have plenty of outdoor space, you could use larger equipment to build larger towers with hollow bricks and cardboard boxes.

Look, listen and note

Does the baby…
- *Follow the movement of the beakers including when they fall down (tracking)?*
- *Respond to and show interest by making familiar sounds, songs and noises?*
- *Use a range of facial expression?*
- *Make noises, bubbles, babbling sounds, chuckling and squealing with delight and anticipation?*
- *Move arms and legs?*
- *Lean forward to grasp and/or pick up a beaker?*
- *How long did they stay engaged (attention span)?*

TOP TIP
Remember to smile and watch for the babies' reactions.

Key words and gestures

- Use of the baby or babies' names
- Names of sounds
- Use gesture and facial expression to reinforce what you say: 'Let's build a tower' 'What's that?' 'What's going to happen to the tower?' 'Oh no, the tower has fallen down' 'What a clever boy/girl you are!' 'Where have they gone?' 'They have crashed' 'One, two, three...' 'Did you hear them crash?' 'You have knocked them over, well done' 'Let's build the tower again' 'What's happening now?' 'One more...'
- Maintain contact with the babies, keep your face where they can see and hear you.

Involving parents

- *Demonstrate and talk to parents about the benefits of buying some stacking beakers and how versatile they are.*
- *Develop a 'Take home sheet' outlining the benefits of stacking beakers, including a selection of songs and rhymes to accompany the activity.*

Extending the challenge

- As you build the tower, move each stacking beaker in front of the baby or babies face to gain their attention and enable them to track the movement of each one.
  - Build the tower on a hard surface to change the sound as the tower falls over.
  - For older babies:
    - Count the beakers as you build the tower.
    - Talk about colours and sizes.
    - Put a smaller beaker inside two larger beakers to make a shaker. Make a variety of sounds quietly and noisily.

Let's have a cuddle

This activity is for one baby of any age!

What you need:

A quiet, warm, safe area for you to sit

You

Enhancing the activity

- Use a soft blanket or shawl to wrap around you both.
- Sit on a blanket on the floor with two babies.

♪ Sing songs. Make one up if you can't remember one or use a nursery rhyme or your own words to a familiar tune such as *Hush a bye baby* or *Miss Polly had a dolly.*

All babies love having a cuddle, and communication improves when babies and children feel secure and safe. A baby can never have too many cuddles! No resources are necessary and a cuddle can be given anywhere. Go on and enjoy this activity!

What you do

1 Carefully pick the baby up, offering head support if necessary.
2 Sit the baby in your lap and gently wrap your arms around the baby saying 'Let's have a lovely cuddle' Some babies may prefer to lie on you, with their head resting on your shoulder while you cuddle them.
3 Talk softly to the baby using their name while stroking their back gently. Keep repeating the baby's name.
4 Sing some lullabies while you gently rock backwards and forwards. Be aware that the baby may fall asleep with the rocking motion.
5 Keep contact with the baby using your warm hands, softly stroking the baby's arms and legs.
6 Talk softly about the baby's day.
7 Once the baby starts to get restless, offer one last cuddle and stop.

Extending the challenge

- Include a teddy bear in the cuddle or a favourite soft toy.
- For older babies:
  - Have a cuddle while on the move, talking about what you can see and what you have done.
  - Respond when babies come to you for a cuddle by putting their arms up to you.
  - Give each other a cuddle to show that adults need them too.
  - Have 'small group' cuddles.

TOP TIP
Make sure you always have time for a cuddle with every baby, every day.

Look, listen and note

Does the baby…
- *Uses body language and sounds to convey likes and dislikes?*
- *Follow your movement and rocking (tracking)*
- *Responds to and show interest with familiar sounds, songs and voices*
- *Have a range of facial expressions?*
- *Makes sounds, bubbles, babbling noises, chuckling and squealing with delight*

Involving parents

- *Display photographs to show parents the enjoyment of this activity.*
- *This should be an enjoyable activity for both baby and parent. Encourage all parents to make time for cuddles.*

Key words and gestures

- Use of the baby's name
- Use gesture and facial expression to reinforce what you say: 'Let's have a cuddle' 'What does that feel like?' 'How nice is that?' 'I like having a cuddle do you?' 'Can you feel the blanket?' 'It feels very soft...' 'Ahhh' 'How soft you are!' 'Lovely' 'Beautiful time' 'What have we done today?' 'We have...'
- Maintain contact with the baby to keep their attention.

Take it outside

- This activity is easily taken outside and some babies respond better there.
- Always check that babies lying on the ground are protected from the sun, from the damp and wind, from other children who may be playing nearby, and from insects or other wildlife.

Pat mats

This activity is for one baby of any age!

What you need:

New zip-lock bags in different sizes (check the zip mechanism to make sure you buy ones with secure zips)

Foam shapes, or shapes cut from polystyrene or foam sheet – foam bath shapes for babies would be good

Food colouring (optional)

Waterproof tape if you are anxious about leakage!

Patting is a natural movement, which all babies use to explore objects, even before they can grasp or poke them. These 'pat mats' are a simple and safe experience for feeling, patting and grasping something soft and interesting. Make sure you use good quality zip-lock bags and check them regularly.

What you do

1 Put some shapes in a zip-lock bag.
2 Add some water and a few drops of food colouring if you like.
3 Zip the bag up, making sure you capture enough air inside to make a soft cushion. Don't over fill the bag or add too much air. The bag should be squeezable without running the risk of bursting the zip. If you want to be extra sure, use waterproof tape to seal the end of the bag.
4 Sit with the baby and explore the bag. Let them pat, squeeze and poke it, and bring it to their mouth.
5 Talk as you explore the bag together, gently describing the objects in the bag and what the baby is doing. Praise the baby for exploring and investigating and for any sounds and babbling.
6 Continue to explore while they are interested.

Involving parents

- This is such a simple activity for parents to do at home. Make sure you give advice on the right sort of bags to use and ideas for safe contents.
- 'Pat mats' are available from toy stores and are a good addition to home toys, or you could add some to your loan collection.

Enhancing the activity

- Make several 'pat mats' with different objects inside. Try adding small soft plastic toys or a bit of bubble mixture.
- Sit on the floor with two babies as you explore more than one mat.

♩ Make up a simple 'Pat Mat song', using the tune of *'Pat-a-Cake'*.
 Pat-a-Cake, Pat-a-Cake pat with your hand.
 Can you feel water or can you feel sand?
 Can you feel shapes as you pat with your hand?
 Pat it and poke it with your little hand.

Take it outside

- This activity is easily taken outside, and some babies respond better there.
- You could add natural materials such as seeds, nuts or leaves to the liquid in the pat mats.
- Babies could explore the bags with bare feet out of doors for a new experience. Hold the babies gently under their arms so their feet can explore the bag.

Extending the challenge

- Offer babies pat mats as they lie on their tummies on a blanket.
- For older babies:
    - Add some tactile materials to the water - beads and sequins, glitter, smooth pebbles or polystyrene packing materials. Make sure the objects have smooth surfaces, so they don't burst the bag.
    - Use an alternative to water – shaving foam, runny custard, tomato sauce, or jelly!

Look, listen and note

Does the baby…
- *Use body language and sounds to convey likes and dislikes?*
- *Follow your movement and the movement of the pat mat (tracking)?*
- *Respond to and shows interest in the contents of the bag?*
- *Makes sounds, bubbles, babbling noises or chuckle and squeal with delight?*

TOP TIP
Clean the outside of the bags after every use.

Key words and gestures

- Can you see?
- Use gesture and facial expression to reinforce what you say: 'Look at the shapes' 'What does that feel like?' 'Can you feel the shapes?' 'Good patting!' 'What's happening now?' 'It feels very squidgy…' 'What's inside?'
- Maintain contact with the baby to keep their attention as they continue to explore.

Let's dance

This activity is suitable for one baby from 3 months to 9 months.

This is a lovely activity to help you to maintain direct contact with the baby as you introduce rhythm and beat. Babies enjoy music and this is a good way to express themselves and to be able to communicate with adults at the same time. There is no right or wrong way of dancing but remember to choose songs carefully from a wide spectrum.

Enhancing the activity

- Dance with a teddy bear or a soft toy.
- With another adult, dance alongside another baby.
- Have some bells and streamers attached to you whilst you dance.

♪ Sing a song – make it up if you can't remember one – or use a nursery rhyme or your own words to a familiar tune such as *This is the way we dance* or *Dance to your Daddy*.

TOP TIP
Be sensitive. Don't have the music on too loud and make sure it is appropriate

What you do

1. Put a CD on and play a song you are familiar with.
2. Have the music playing loud enough for the baby to hear.
3. Pick the baby up and hold them close to you, saying 'Shall we dance?'
4. Remember to support the baby's head if needed.
5. Gently move around the room as you listen to the music together.
6. Use plenty of facial expressions and eye contact with the baby as you dance, emphasising your voice as you hum or sing.
7. Watch for the baby's reactions and if they are happy, put on a different song and dance again.
8. Carefully lift the baby high in the air in time with the music.
9. Once the baby becomes restless, stop dancing and have a cuddle.

Key words and gestures

- Use of the baby's name
- Toy and object names
- Names of sounds
- Repeated sound and rhythmical phrases help babie's language to develop
- Use gesture and facial expression to reinforce what you say: 'What's that?' 'Shall we dance?' 'Let's put on some music' 'Can you hear the music?' 'Is it loud, quiet...?' 'This is fun' 'I like dancing do you?' 'Can you hear the beat?' 'Let's do it together' 'Are you smiling? What a lovely smile' 'Let's dance around the room' 'This is my favourite song'
- Don't talk so much that the baby can't concentrate on the music and rhythm!

Look, listen and note

Does the baby…
- *Respond to sounds, songs and voices?*
- *Makes sounds, bubbles or babbling noises?*
- *Begin to move in time to adult movement or music, moving their head or waving their arms and hands?*
- *Express fun and enjoyment through smiles and laughter?*

Involving parents

- *Take some photos and display them, so parents can see how you do the activity and the enjoyment of music.*
- *Do a 'Take home sheet' of suitable songs from around the world to dance to.*
- *Ask parents to bring in music from their home and their background.*

Take it outside

- If possible, take the music outside and enjoy dancing around the garden. Follow your Health and Safety policy when taking electrical items outside.
- Always check to be sure babies are protected from the sun, from the damp and wind, from other children who may be playing nearby, and from insects and other wildlife.

Extending the challenge

- Use a variety of music, introducing different beats and rhythm from around the world.
- Sit with the baby on your lap and clap in time with the beat.
- Encouraging group dancing with all the children.
- For older babies:
  - Standing up, hold their hands while they dance.
  - As the activity becomes familiar, older babies will respond to songs they like and dislike.
  - Introduce musical instruments.
  - Add some props – different types of hats, glasses and clothes.

Nursery rhymes

This activity is suitable for one baby from birth.

Nursery rhymes are a favourite for babies and an excellent way of introducing new words and sounds from a very young age. There are many nursery rhyme books avaliable that will encourage everyone in your setting to use rhymes with babies. Collect plenty of these and make sure they are where everyone can access them.

Enhancing the activity

- Use a mirror to observe the baby's responses.
- Each time you change the baby, sing their favourite nursery rhyme.

♪ Sing any gentle songs and lullabies such as: *Hush a bye baby, Miss Polly had a dolly, Humpty Dumpty* or *Twinkle twinkle little star.*

What you do

1. Sit comfortably, holding the baby and ensuring their head is fully supported.
2. Make sure that the baby can gaze into your face with ease and is near enough to see you, (20 to 35 cm is a good distance).
3. Softly start to sing some nursery rhymes to the baby.
4. Use lots of voice tone to emphasize key words of each nursery rhyme.
5. Rock gently backwards and forwards as you sing, while softly cuddling the baby.
6. If using a nursery rhyme book, share the book with the baby showing the illustration, but don't forget the power of eye contact!
7. Use plenty of facial expression and eye contact with the baby.
8. Observe the baby's reactions and praise them when they respond.
9. Repeat the nursery rhymes especially if there has been a positive response from the baby.

Key words and gestures

- Use of the baby's name
- Toy and object names
- Names of sounds
- Repeated sound and rhythmical phrases help babie's language to develop.
- Use gesture and facial expression to reinforce what you say: 'What's that?' 'Shall we sing some songs?' 'Which rhymes shall we sing?' 'Let's sing quietly or loudly' 'Did you enjoy that?' 'I did' 'Let's look in the nursery rhyme book' 'Look' 'Listen' 'Can you hear me?'
- Keep your face where they can see you – eye contact is vital for good early communication!

Look, listen and note

Does the baby…
- *Follows your movements with their gaze (tracking)?*
- *Respond to sounds, songs and voices?*
- *Makes sounds, bubbles and babbling noises?*
- *Reach out to touch your face, hands and fingers?*
- *Smile with enjoyment?*

TOP TIP

Don't worry about your singing voice, babies just love being sung too!

Take it outside

- Nursery rhyme sessions are easily transferred to your outside area.
- Always check to be sure babies are protected from the sun, from the damp and wind, from other children who may be playing nearby, and from insects or other wildlife.
- Sing songs associated with outdoors such as *It's raining, it's pouring* or *Two little dickie birds*.

Involving parents

- *Contribute their own childhood rhymes to a nursery rhyme booklet for parents to use at home.*
- *Use every day occurrences to sing to the baby, such as nappy time, trips in the car etc.*

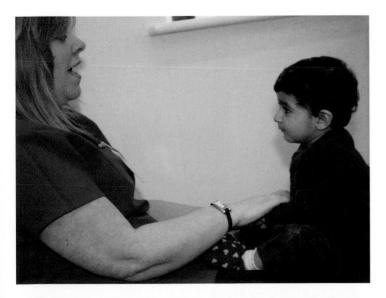

Extending the challenge

- Use pictures or objects to enhance the nursery rhymes.
- Sing songs linked to events such as seasons, birthdays.
- For older babies:
    - Have a small group of babies singing together
    - Let them choose which nursery rhymes they want to sing.
    - Collect and sing action songs, and counting songs.

Pat-a-cake

This activity is suitable for one baby from birth.

What you need:

Comfortable chair

Bells to tie on your wrist

A mirror

Enhancing the activity

- Use a larger mirror so the baby will be able to see you and your facial expression.
- Use a favourite toy for the baby to sing with.

♪ Sing a song whenever you feel like it! Sing any baby nursery rhyme or your own words to a familiar tune such as *Miss Polly had a dolly* or *Wind the bobbin*.

Singing *Pat-a-cake* to the baby will ensure that you have quality one to one time using an old favourite nursery rhyme. It's a lovely relaxing song with an easy beat that can be sung from birth, but is equally enjoyed by older babies.

What you do

1 Sit with the baby and carefully position them so they are facing away from you.
2 Position the mirror opposite you so you can see the baby's face.
3 Talk softly to the baby as you gently stroke their face, making them feel safe and secure.
4 Talk to the baby: 'Let's sing Pat-a-cake'.
5 Quietly sing 'Pat-a-cake' while you clap your hands softly in front of the baby.
6 At the end of the song, gently tickle the baby's tummy in delight.
7 Once the baby is familiar with the song, strap the bells to your wrist and sing the song again.
8 Encourage the baby to reach out and touch the bells, as well as your hands and fingers.
9 Using the mirror, observe the baby's responses and when it's time to finish singing, pick the baby up, give them a cuddle and praise them.

Take it outside

- Always check to be sure babies lying on the ground are protected from the sun, from the damp and wind, from other children who may be playing nearby, and from insects or other wildlife.
- Put a blanket on a waterproof picnic blanket in a shady, safe place on the grass under a tree and have a rhyme time.
- Be aware of the sun reflecting in mirrors out of doors.

Look, listen and note

Does the baby…

- *Show head control by raising his/her head up and down and from side to side?*
- *Respond to sounds, songs and voices?*
- *Make sounds, coos, bubbles, babbling noises, and laughter?*
- *Smile and kick with enjoyment?*
- *Watch and follow the movement of your hands (tracking)?*
- *Reach out?*

Key words and gestures

- Use of the baby or babies' name
- Toy and object names
- Names of sounds
- Repeated sound and rhythmical phrases help babie's language to develop
- Use gesture and facial expression to reinforce what you say: 'What a beautiful baby you are!' 'Look at that lovely smile' 'I can hear you. What are you telling me?' 'That's right' 'Look at the mirror. Is it shiny?' 'Shall we do some singing?' 'Are you ready?' 'Let's sing quietly...softy...loudly 'Let's do it again' 'Did you enjoy that?' 'Can you hear me?' 'Can you do it?' 'Look' 'Listen' 'Let's...'

Involving parents

- *Take some photos and display them, so parents can see the responses of the babies during the singing session.*
- *Develop an action rhyme booklet for parents to use at home.*
- *Use everyday occurrences to make simple songs to sing to the baby, including at nappy time.*

Extending the challenge

- Try different rhythms and speeds – quickly, slowly using a range of voice tones and volumes.
- For older babies:
  - Babies that can sit unaided can do the actions together on a blanket.
  - Include a favourite soft toy and let the baby sing *Pat-a-Cake* to the toy.
  - Tie bells on baby's own wrists or ankles.

TOP TIP
Use bells and wristbands that are made specially for babies.

Action songs

This activity is suitable for one baby from birth to 20 months.

What you need:

Changing mat

Quiet changing area

Songs and rhymes are a well-tried way of communicating with babies, and nappy time should be a very happy and relaxed activity for both adults and babies. You can sing songs at any time of the day with babies, but here the activity focuses on songs at nappy time.

Enhancing the activity

- Any songs can be used including *This little piggy* and *Five little ducks*.
- Be creative and make up your own songs or new versions. Write these in a notebook so you can all use them.
- Use a blanket instead of the changing mat, which will allow more than one baby to join in this activity.

♩ Sing a song about the toy – make it up if you can't remember one – or use a nursery rhyme or your own words to a familiar tune such as *Teddy bear, teddy bear, touch your nose*.

What you do

1. After you have finished changing the baby, leave him/her on the changing mat and where possible, not fully dressed – just in their nappy and vest so they can move freely.
2. Make sure the changing mat or changing table is in a safe and warm area.
3. Sit or stand at the end of the changing mat and make sure your hands are warm.
4. Talk to the baby about what you are going to do, 'Shall we sing some songs now?' 'Are you ready...?'
5. Start with a favourite such as *The Grand Old Duke of York*. As you sing this song, move the baby's legs gently up and down in time with the tune of the song.
6. At the end of the song, grab the baby's feet softly and tickle them asking them: 'Did you enjoy that?'
7. Now try *Round and round the garden* Start this song by using the babies hands and end with a gentle tickle under the arms. You can sing again, starting with their feet and ending with a tickle at the tops of their legs.
8. During your singing use plenty of large hand, arm and finger gestures, and anticipation, and watch how the baby follows your body movements.
9. Use plenty of eye contact, voice tone and facial expressions during the singing to keep the baby interested.
10. Observe the baby's responses and repeat the song if the baby is happy.
11. When the baby has lost interest, ask them 'Have we finished singing.' 'Shall we go and...?'
12. Pick the baby up and give them a cuddle and a tickle before taking them to another place to play.

TOP TIP
Use a song book to remind you of different songs and to introduce new ones.

Extending the challenge

- Sing the songs differently – quickly, slowly, loudly and softly.
- Include musical instruments.
- For older babies:
  - Sit two babies facing each other holding hands and sing *Row, row, row your boat*. You should be next to them in case they need to be supported.
  - Include a teddy bear or favourite soft toy.

Look, listen and note

Does the baby…
- *Make sounds, coos, bubbles, babbling noises or chuckles and squeals of delight?*
- *Show interest in listening to a range of songs and sounds?*
- *Smile and kick with enjoyment?*
- *Move fingers, hands and arms?*
- *Watch the movements of adult hands and fingers (tracking)?*
- *Reach out and try to hold adult hands and fingers?*

Take it outside

- Although nappy time may be difficult to do outside, the concept of lying down alongside a baby or babies is still very manageable out of doors.
- Always check to be sure babies lying on the ground are protected from the sun, from the damp and wind, from other children who may be playing nearby, and from insects or other wildlife.
- Put the blanket on a waterproof picnic blanket in a shady, safe place on the grass under a tree or bush so they can watch and listen to the leaves as you sing.

Involving parents

- *Use displays within the environment to demonstrate to parents the importance of singing and action songs for babies.*
- *Develop a song sheet for parents to take home including the tunes of the songs.*

Key words and gestures

- Use of the baby's or babies' name
- Toy and object names
- Names of sounds
- Repeated sound and rhythmical phrases help babies language to develop
- Use gesture and facial expression to reinforce what you say: 'Shall we do some singing?' 'What songs shall we sing today?' 'We like to sing…' 'Are you ready…?' 'You are beautiful…' 'Shall we do it again?' 'Let's sing the song quietly or loudly.' 'How many songs shall we sing today?' 'Are you kicking?' 'Lots of fun…'
- Maintain contact with the babies and use different voice tones to keep their attention

Giddy up!

This activity is suitable for one baby from six months.

What you need:

A warm, safe area on the floor large enough for you to lie down

Enhancing the activity

- Take a teddy bear or favourite toy on the adventure.

- ♪ Sing a song – make it up if you can't remember one – or use a nursery rhyme or your own words to a familiar tune such as *Horsey, horsey don't you stop* or *Ride a cock horse*.

This activity is great fun for both you and the baby, and is especially enjoyed by dads and older brothers and sisters. Going for a 'horse ride' is a perfect opportunity to communicate with the baby while using beat and rhythm to express your language and movements.

What you do

1 Lie on your back with your legs bent to protect your back. Sit the baby on your tummy, using your thighs to help support them.
2 Hold the baby under his/her arms and ensure they has full head control.
3 Gain the baby's attention by saying his/her name.
4 Smile while you talk to the baby about the 'horse ride adventure' you are about to go on.
5 Gently, move your body as you go on your horse ride:
   - Up and down: 'The horse is walking over the grass – swish, swish'.
   - Sideways: 'The horse is going through a river – splash, splash'.
   - Up and down slowly: 'The horse is going through some mud – squelch, squelch'.
   - Bumping gently: 'The horse is going over some rocks – crash, bang'.
   - Lift your legs up and down, tapping your feet 'The horse is going over a bridge – trip trap, trip trap''.
   - Up and down quickly: 'The horse is galloping – giddy up giddy up'.
6 Maintain eye contact with the baby and use plenty of voice tone to emphasize the different sounds, beat and situations.
7 Watch the baby and observe how they are responding to the different movements.
8 Carry on and repeat if the baby is still enjoying the adventure.

Take it outside

- On a warm dry day, this 'adventure' can easily happen outside on a rug or the grass.
- Take the 'adventure' around the garden by holding the baby in your arms and exploring the outdoor environment as you move quickly or slowly.
- Always check to be sure babies are protected from the sun, from the damp and wind, from other children who may be playing nearby, and from insects or other wildlife.

Look, listen and note

Does the baby…
- *Respond to sounds, songs and voices?*
- *Make sounds, babbling noises and laughter?*
- *Kick and smile with full enjoyment?*
- *Chuckle and squeal with delight?*
- *Stay engaged (for how long)?*

Key words and gestures

- Use of the baby's or babies' name
- Names of sounds
- Repeated sound and rhythmical phrases help babie's language to develop
- Use gesture and facial expression to reinforce what you say: 'Are you ready?' 'Let's go' 'Horse' 'Neigh neigh' 'Splash, splosh, splash' 'Squelch' 'Trip trap, trip trap' 'Giddy up!' 'Bang bang' 'Are you having fun?' 'Let's do it together' 'You are funny' 'What can we see, some grass…'
- Maintain contact with the baby and use different voice tones to keep his/her attention.

Involving parents

- *Demonstrate to parents how to do this 'adventure' and share with them associated nursery rhymes.*
- *Dads really enjoy this activity, but you may need to remind them to be gentle!*

Extending the challenge

- Show the baby picture books and photos of horses.
- Use different beats and timings on the 'adventure'.
- Use coconut shells to represent the sound of horseshoes.
- For younger babies:
  - Sit the baby in your lap and go on the adventure. Be gentle.
  - Clap your hands and tap your feet.
- For older babies:
  - Put various materials into containers for the babies to touch and explore – grass, mud, water and rocks.

TOP TIP
Use your imagination and be creative – take the 'adventure' anywhere!

Baby dance

This activity is suitable for babies from 6 months in a group.

What you need:

An adult for every baby

A warm, safe area large enough to move about in

'Baby dance' will introduce rhythm to the babies by moving together to a range of different beats, rhythms and music. A sense of rhythm is essential for speaking and listening, as it introduces babies to the rhythms of language through music. For 'Baby dance', you will need one adult for every baby and it's also important that the babies can hold their heads well.

Enhancing the activity

• Do the same dance with the babies facing away from the adults and working in pairs so the babies can see each other.

♪ Sing a song or use a nursery rhyme or your own words to familiar tunes: *This is the way we dance, Here we go Looby Lou, Ring-o-roses, Round* and *round the village.*

What you do

1 Make a circle with each adult standing and holding the baby facing them, supporting the baby under their arms.
2 Move around the circle taking steady side steps and sing together, using a tune you are comfortable with:
   Step and step, 1, 2 , 3, step and step, dance with me,
   Step and step, 1, 2, 3, step and stop and look at me.
3 On the last line, stop suddenly, swing the babies gently high in the air, hold them there, maintain eye contact for a moment before swinging them gently down again.
4 Continue the dance, observing the babies' reactions.
5 Stop when they have had enough and give them a cuddle.

Extending the challenge

• Use a range of beats and tunes.
• Introduce musical instruments, wrist bells or ribbons.
• For older babies:
   · Quicken the pace and make the game livelier.
   · Dance with the babies standing up, holding their hands while they dance.
   · As the activity becomes familiar, older babies will respond to songs they like and dislike.

Look, listen and note

Does the baby…
- *Make large movements of his/her arms and legs?*
- *Respond to sounds, songs and voices?*
- *Make sounds, bubbles or babbling noises?*
- *Reach out to touch your face, hands and fingers?*
- *Maintain eye contact and attention when in the air?*
- *Anticipate the lift into the air by wriggling or laughing?*
- *Smile with enjoyment?*

Key words and gestures

- Use of the baby's or babies' name
- Repeated sound and rhythmical phrases help babies language to develop
- Use gesture and facial expression to reinforce what you say: 'What's that?' 'Shall we dance?' 'Let's put on some music' "Can you hear the music?' 'This is fun' 'I like dancing, do you?' 'Can you hear the beat?' 'Let's do it together' 'Are you smiling? What a lovely smile!' 'Let's dance around the room' 'This is my favourite song'
- Keep your face where they can see you – so they can focus.

Involving parents

- *Demonstrate to parents how much babies love music and love to dance.*
- *Display photographs of the babies dancing, along with a selection of suitable music*
- *Bring in music from home.*

TOP TIP
You can do Baby Dance with just you and one baby as you move around the setting.

Take it outside

- You have the freedom to move about outside with no restrictions, so 'Baby dance' should be even more fun out of doors.
- Always check to be sure babies are protected from the sun, from the damp and wind, from other children who may be playing nearby, and from insects or other wildlife.

Stories at nappy time

This activity is suitable for one or two babies from 4 months to 20 months.

What you need:

Changing mats

Quiet changing area

Selection of appropriate board or baby books. To build up your confidence, get familiar with the books before you use them with the babies

Enhancing the activity

- Use a variety of different types of books.
- Use a blanket instead of the changing mat.
- Make up your own stories, such as 'What have we done today?'

♪ Sing associated songs, linking them to the books you are currently using with the baby or babies.
♪ Get hold of some song storybooks or rhyming stories.

Stories can and should be a daily experience for all babies from a very young age. Books enable you to talk to the babies and are a great way of building and developing relationships between adult and baby.

What you do

1 After you have finished changing a baby, leave his/her on the changing mat and where possible, don't get the baby fully dressed. Leave his/her just in their nappy and vest so they can wave and kick freely.
2 Talk to the baby about what you are going to do, 'Let's look at this book. Let's have a story.'
3 Place a cushion next to the changing mat and lie down next to the baby ensuring your head is next to the his/her head. If you have two babies, lie down between the two babies.
4 Have a selection of appropriate board books next to you, including some quieter stories such as 'Guess How Much I Love You'.
5 Choose a book and hold it in front of the baby or babies making sure they can see the book and each page.
6 Start to read the book, using a variety of voice tones and making frequent eye contact with each baby.
7 Encourage them to reach out and touch the book. Even at this young age, feely books are a good way to introduce textures and materials.
8 When you have finished the book, talk about the book 'Did you enjoy that? 'What a lovely story'.
9 If they are still interested and happy, move on to the next book. Observe their responses and stop when they have had enough.
10 When the baby has lost interest, ask his/her 'Have we finished looking at books, what shall we do now?' 'Shall we go...?.'
11 Pick the baby or babies up and give them a cuddle and a tickle before moving on to the next activity.

Take it outside

- Although nappy time may be difficult to do outside, the concept of lying down alongside a baby or babies is still very manageable out of doors.
- Always check to be sure babies lying on the ground are protected from the sun, from the damp and wind, from other children who may be playing nearby, and from insects or other wildlife.
- Put a blanket on a waterproof picnic blanket in a shady, safe place on the grass under a tree or bush so they can watch and listen to the leaves and the sounds as you read stories together.

Look, listen and note

Does the baby…
- *Make sounds, coos, bubbles, babbling noises or chuckles and squeals of delight?*
- *Show interest in listening to a range of songs and stories?*
- *Smile and kick with enjoyment?*
- *Move fingers, hands and arms?*
- *Watch the movements of your hands and fingers (tracking)?*
- *Reach out and try to hold the book?*

Key words and gestures

- Use of the baby's or babies' name
- Repeated sound and rhythmical phrases help babies language to develop
- Use gesture and facial expression to reinforce what you say: 'Lets have a story?' 'What's that?' 'What book shall we look at now?' 'Did you enjoy the story book?' 'Well done, you are a clever girl/boy!' 'What does that feel like?' 'Look at the beautiful book' 'How many books shall we look at today?' 'I love books'
- Maintain contact with the babies and use different voice tones to keep their attention.

Involving parents

- *You could make a display in your setting to demonstrate to parents the importance of books for babies.*
- *Encourage parents to bring favourite stories and books from home.*
- *Start a book library encouraging parents to borrow books and read at home.*
- *Share information with parents about local libraries and facilities available to them including 'Story time' at the library and the Bookstart project.*

Extending the challenge

- Read more than one book in every session, making sure you choose contrasting types and individual babies' favourites. Even very young babies can show you which books these are.
- Add some nursery rhyme books.
- For older babies:
  - Take babies and children to visit your local library.
  - Introduce longer, more complex stories.
  - Use story aids such as soft toys and other familiar objects.

TOP TIP
Share the love of books with babies from a very young age - a baby is never too young to experience books

Home made books

This activity is suitable for one baby from 3 month.

What you need:

A4 white and black card

Scissors

Glue (child safe)

Hole punch

Piece of ribbon or wool

Laminator and laminator pouches (if available)

Enhancing the activity

- Hang the book on a baby gym/activity mat.
- Include a black and white soft toy.
- Share the book with two babies sitting in chairs together.

♩ Sing a song. Make it up if you can't remember one or use a nursery rhyme or your own words to a familiar tune. Made up songs don't have to be complicated:
*Black and white, black and white
See my book is black and white.
Black and white, black and white
My book's black and white.*
(Sing to the tune of *This old man*)

Making your own books for babies is not only fun, but also very rewarding and can be inexpensive. In this activity, using contrasting black and white patterns will stimulate babies from a very early age.

What you do

1 Cut out various shapes (zigzag, spots and strips) from the black and white card.
2 Stick the black shapes on pages of white card and the white shapes on pages of black card.
3 If you have access to a laminator, laminate the pieces of card to make them last longer.
4 Hole punch the cards and tie securely together with a piece of ribbon or wool, making sure you can still open the pages.
5 Once the glue is dry, introduce the baby to the book.
6 Sit comfortably with the baby, ensuring you support his/her head.
7 Talk and smile to the baby as you introduce the book of patterns. Remember a good distance for a baby to focus on is about 22 cm.
8 Use plenty of facial expression and eye contact with the baby as you show the patterns, changing your voice tone as you introduce each page.
9 Watch for the baby's reactions. If they reach out, let them touch and feel the book.
10 Once the baby becomes restless, put the book away and give him/her a cuddle.

Key words and gestures

- Use of the baby's or babies' name
- Repeated sound and rhythmical phrases help babies' language to develop
- Use gesture and facial expression to reinforce what you say – 'What's that?' 'Shall we have a look at the book?' 'Can you see the patterns?' 'What can you see?' 'Look, it's black, white, stripy, zigzag, spotty.' 'Do you want to touch it?' 'What a clever boy you are' 'Lets turn the page' 'What does that feel like?' 'Soft, hard' 'Look'

Look, listen and note

Does the baby…
- *Respond to sounds, songs and voices?*
- *Make sounds, bubbles or babbling noises?*
- *Grasp, kick and reach?*
- *Have good head control?*
- *Show enjoyment with smiles and laughter?*

Extending the challenge

- Use different textures, such as black fur on white card, or black fur and white bubble wrap for a feely black and white book.
- Attach a bell to the book for sounds.
- For older babies:
    - Let the babies hold the book themselves.
    - Let them help you to make their own books, by offering them ready cut shapes and using the ones they select to make the book.
    - Use an unbreakable mirror for reflections and patterns.
    - Use black shapes on white paper plates to make faces.

Take it outside

- Taking books outside extends the value of books (SF?) and it's lovely to have time outside sharing books together in a quiet spot.
- Always check to be sure babies are protected from the sun, from the damp and wind, from other children who may be playing nearby, and from insects and other wildlife.

Involving parents

- Take some photos and display them along with examples of the books. Parents can see how to do the activity and how they can make a book at home.

TOP TIP

Be creative – don't throw any odd bits of black and white card away. Make some interesting patterns in these home made books.

'Dear Zoo'

This activity is suitable for one baby from birth.

What you need:

Somewhere comfortable to sit

A warm quiet area with minimum disruptions – a settee or comfortable armchair would be ideal!

'*Dear Zoo*' by Rod Campbell (board book version)

Enhancing the activity

- Use a mirror to observe the baby's responses. If you mount a mirror permanently on the wall at floor height in your setting, you will find it very useful for all sorts of baby activities.

- ♪ Sing a song such as: *Daddy's taking us to the zoo tomorrow, Down in the jungle, An elephant goes like this and that, Mmm, mmm went the little green frog, Five little monkeys*, or *Alice the Camel*

It's never too early to start reading books to babies and to share the love of books with them. Reading books is a great way of communicating and 'Dear Zoo' is a classic first book to share with a baby.

What you do

1 Sit comfortably holding the baby, ensuring their head is fully supported and he/she can see your face as well as the book.
2 Say the baby's name to gain their attention and show them the cover of the book 'Look shall we look at this book, its *Dear Zoo*.'
3 Ensure that the baby can see you and the book with ease. (20 to 35 cm is a good distance).
4 Start to read the text slowly and allow plenty of time for each page.
5 Carefully lift the flap on each page showing each animal picture. Quietly make the animal noises.
6 Use lots of voice tone to emphasize key words, such as 'So I sent him back'.
7 Use plenty of facial expression and make frequent eye contact with the baby.
8 Encourage the baby to reach and touch the book and praise for their efforts.
9 Observe the baby's responses and repeat the story if he/she is content.
10 Finish the story with a cuddle.

Extending the challenge

- Find some pictures or photographs of the animals.
- Use visual aids to enhance the book – soft toys of the animals.
- For older babies:
  - Have a small group of babies and read the book as a group.
  - Take the children to visit to local library.
  - Encourage the babies to look at the books by themselves.
  - Dress up as animals with masks or tails and ears on headbands.

Look, listen and note

Does the baby…
* *Follow the movements with their gaze (tracking)?*
* *Respond to sounds, songs and voices?*
* *Makes sounds, bubbles, babbling noises?*
* *Reach out to touch the book?*
* *Smile and kick with enjoyment?*

Key words and gestures

* Use of the baby's or babies' name
* Names of sounds
* Repeated sound and rhythmical phrases help babie's language to develop
* Use gesture and facial expression to reinforce what you say: 'Shall we look at some books?' 'Which books shall we read?' 'Let's turn the page' 'Did you enjoy that?' 'What a lovely story' 'Shall we look at another book?' 'That's lovely having a cuddle' 'Did you enjoy that?' 'I did' 'Look' 'Listen' 'Can you hear me?'
* Keep your face where they can see you – you need to be close!

Involving parents

* *Display suitable books for babies where parents can look at them.*
* *Loan books for parents to use at home.*
* *Share information about local libraries and Book Start.*

Take it outside

* Stories are easily transferred to a quiet corner outside.
* Always check to be sure babies are protected from the sun, from the damp and wind, from other children who may be playing nearby, and from insects or other wildlife.
* Read books associated with outdoors e.g. *We're Going on a Bear Hunt* or *The Gruffalo*.

TOP TIP
Although this book is fairly short, take your time and enjoy it with the baby. It will soon become a favourite!

'Hairy MacLary'

This activity is suitable for one or two babies from 3 months.

Enhancing the activity

- Use a soft toy dog.

♪ Sing songs about the books you have read. If you can't remember a suitable song, make one up, or have a song book at hand to look at: *How much is that doggy in the window? Oh where, oh where has my little dog gone? The farmer's dog's at my back door*

Introducing rhymes and rhyming text to babies from an early age will develop an awareness of rhythm and rhyme within their speech, and there are now hundreds of rhyming board books for babies. *Hairy MacLary from Donaldson's Dairy* **is a lovely rhyming book.** *More adventures of Hairy MacLary* **are also available in board book format.**

What you do

1 Sit in a comfortable chair with one or two babies.
2 Tuck the babies into your arms, so you can support their heads.
3 Hold the book in front of them ensuring that they can gaze into the book with ease (20 to 35 cm is a good distance).
4 Gain the babies' attention by using their names and introduce the book 'Look what I have. Let's look at *Hairy MacLary from Donaldson's Dairy*'.
5 Look at the book together. Slowly start to read the text allowing plenty of time for each page.
6 Use voice tone and emphasize the rhyming text.
7 Encourage the babies to reach out and touch the book. Praise them for their efforts.
8 After reading the book once, repeat the story but this time, stop at each page to look at the pictures in more depth.
9 As you finish the book, give the babies a hug.
10 If they are content, choice another rhyming book such as *'Peepo'*, *'Monkey Puzzle'* or *'The Gruffalo'*.

Key words and gestures

- Use of the baby's or babies' name
- Use gesture and facial expression to reinforce what you say: 'Shall we look at some books?' 'Do you like dogs?' 'What noises do they make?' 'Bark' 'Woof' 'Which books shall we read?' 'Let's turn the page' 'Did you enjoy that?' 'What a lovely story' 'Shall we look at another book?' 'That's lovely having a cuddle' 'Did you enjoy that?' 'I did' 'Look' 'Listen' 'Can you hear me?'
- Maintain contact with the baby and use different voice tones to keep their attention.

Look, listen and note

Does the baby…
- *Focus on you?*
- *Reach out to touch and grasp?*
- *Make sounds, coos, bubbles, babbling noises, chuckles and squeals?*
- *Smile with enjoyment?*
- *Kick with excitement?*
- *Attention span – how long did he/she stay engaged?*

Take it outside

- Stories are easily transferred to outside. Take a basket of books and a rug and sit outside in the shade or a sheltered place – you could even sit in a pop-up tent!
- Always check to be sure babies are protected from the sun, from the damp and wind, from other children who may be playing nearby, and from insects or other wildlife.
- Read books associated with outdoors e.g. *We're going on a bear hunt* or *The Gruffalo*.

Extending the challenge

- Put a mirror in front of you so you can see the babies' responses and they can see you.
- Use a different voice tone for different parts of the book - quieter, louder – and add some character voices.
- For older babies:
  - Have a number of rhyming books and encourage the babies to choose which book they want to listen to.
  - Make up simple rhymes.
  - Up the tempo of the rhyming text.

TOP TIP
Be familiar with the rhyming books before you start!

Involving parents

- Ask parents to bring in a pet dog if they have one – follow your health and safety policy.
- Display suitable books for babies and show to parents.
- Loan books for parents to use at home.
- Share information about local libraries and Book Start.

What we did today

This activity is suitable for one baby from 6 months.

What you need:

A comfortable chair/cushions

A quiet, warm environment with minimum disruptions

Telling stories without a book is an activity that all practitioners should learn to do. One easy way to start making these stories is to use the events of the day. Towards the end of the day, it's lovely to talk to the baby about what they have done and with a bit of imagination, 'What we did today' can easily become a story.

Enhancing the activity

- Where possible show items associated with the day – a favourite toy or photographs

- ♪ Sing songs about what you have seen. If you can't remember one, make up a song or have a song book at hand to look at e.g. *This is the way we...*

What you do

1 Find somewhere comfortable to sit with the baby. Sideways on your lap is a good position so you can maintain physical contact with them and they can see your face.
2 Call the baby's name to get his/her attention.
3 Talk gently to the baby about their day. Think about:
   - the sequence of the day
   - activities they have enjoyed
   - meal times
   - friends they have played with
   - indoor and outdoor play.
4 Use plenty of facial expression and smiles as you tell the 'story'.
5 Use a range of voice tones to keep his/her interested and to emphasise aspects of the day.
6 Maintain eye contact with the baby and observe their reactions.
7 Allow time for the baby to respond to you – praise them for their efforts.
8 Share 'What we did today' with parents.

Extending the challenge

- Turn 'What we did today' into a song or rhyme, using a tune such as '*Here we go round the Mulberry Bush*'.
- Go outside when talking about the outdoor play activities.
- Use visual prompts.
- For older babies:
   - Change the sequence of the day.
   - Ask the babies what they did today.

Look, listen and note

Does the baby…
- *Reach out to touch and grasp?*
- *Make sounds, coos, bubbles, babbling noises or chuckles and squeals?*
- *Smile with enjoyment?*
- *Kick and move his/her arms with delight?*
- *Respond to sounds and voices?*
- *Focus? For how long?*

Key words and gestures

- Use of the baby's or babies' name
- Use gesture and facial expression to reinforce what you say: 'What have we done today?' 'Let's think' 'Can you remember when you did?' 'We've had a lovely day 'This morning, this afternoon…'
- Maintain contact with the baby and use different voice tones to keep his/her attention

Take it inside

- Stories are easily transferred to outside. Sit comfortably on some cushions.
- Always check to be sure babies are protected from the sun, from the damp and wind, from other children who may be playing nearby and from insects or other wildlife.

TOP TIP
Make sure you know what each of your key group of babies have done today.

Involving parents

- Share the 'What we did today' story with parents.
- Share with parents the importance of talking to babies and how 'What we did today' can be part of the journey home.

Tell me a story

This activity is suitable for one baby from 6 months.

What you need:

Comfortable chair

It's very rewarding to make up stories using your imagination and being creative. Babies will respond to you talking and will enjoy hearing their name within the story.

Enhancing the activity

- A large mirror so the baby will be able to see you and your facial expressions.

♪ Sing songs about what you have seen. If you can't remember one, make up a song or have a songbook at hand to look at e.g. *This is the way we...*

TOP TIP

Keep using the baby's name within the story!

What you do

1 Sit with the baby comfortably on a chair and make sure she/he is well supported in your arms.
2 Softly talk to the baby as you gently stroke his/her face making his/her feel safe and secure.
3 Carefully position the baby so they are facing towards you.
4 Talk to the baby 'Let's have a story about you'.
5 Look around the environment for ideas:
   - What's the weather doing?
   - What's the baby wearing?
   - Who else is around – adults and friends?
   - Favourite toys.
6 Personalise the story and involve family members.
7 Smile and use plenty of facial expression and voice tone.
8 During the story, offer a hug and a tickle to maintain contact.
9 Allow time for the baby to join in the story and communicate back to you. Praise them for their communication.
10 Observe the baby's responses and when it's time, finish the story with a lovely ending and pick the baby up and give a cuddle.

Take it outside

- This is a perfect activity to take outside.
  Some babies really love being out of doors and will really enjoy 'Tell me a story' outside on a blanket on a waterproof picnic blanket in a shady, safe place on the grass under a tree or bush.
- Always check to be sure babies are protected from the sun, from the damp and wind, from other children who may be playing nearby and from insects or other wildlife.

Look, listen and note

Does the baby...
- *Respond to sounds, songs and voices?*
- *Make sounds, coos, bubbles, babbling noises or laughter?*
- *Smile and kick with enjoyment?*
- *Follow the movement of your body and face (tracking)?*
- *Reach out?*

Key words and gestures

- Use of the baby's or babies' name
- Names of sounds
- Repeated sound and rhythmical phrases help babies' language to develop
- Use gesture and facial expression to reinforce what you say: 'Let's go on a journey' 'What a beautiful baby you are!' 'Look at that lovely smile' 'I can hear you' 'What are you telling me?' 'That's right' 'Look at the mirror. Is it shiny?' 'Are you ready?' 'Let's do it again' 'Did you enjoy that?' 'Can you hear me?' 'Look' 'Listen' 'Let's...'
- Maintain contact with the baby and use different voice tones to keep his/her attention

Extending the challenge

- Take a favourite soft toy with you for the story.
- Use favourite books, objects and pictures to enhance these personal stories.
- For older babies:
    - Let them join in the story and introduce their own ideas.
    - Do some mark making around the story.
    - Go outside – bring in textures of plants and the weather (Follow your health and safety policy on safty with plants.)

Involving parents

Talk to parents about using their imagination to 'Tell a story', particularly at bedtime, when babies and children really benefit from re-visiting the events of the day.

Books and songs

Babies from birth will enjoy the experience of books and a baby is never too young to share a book with a familiar adult.

At this age, board books and material books are most appropriate and suited and you can easily obtain favourite stories in board board versions.

Before you read a book with a baby, ensure that you and the baby are sitting comfortably in a warm, quiet environment and that you are familiar with the book before you start.

A selection of suitable books:

Dear Zoo by Rod Campbell
(Campbell Books)

We're Going on a Bear Hunt by Michael Rosen
and Helen Oxenbury
(Walker Books)

The Gruffalo by Julia Donaldson and
Alex Scheffler
(Macmillian)

Monkey Puzzle by Julia Donaldson and
Alex Scheffler
(Campbell Books)

Owl Babies by Martin Waddle
(Walker Books)

Noisy Farm by Rod Campbell
(Campbell Books)

Harry Maclary from Donaldson Dairy
– Lynley Dodd
(Puffin Books)

Peepo by Janet and Allan Ahlberg
(Penguin Books)

The Very Hungry Caterpillar by Eric Carle
(Penguin Books)

Baby Faces
(DK Publishing)

Touch and Feel: Farm
(DK Publishing)

Who's Hiding Under the Sea? by Debbie Tarbett
(Little Tiger Press)

Guess How Much I Love You by Sam McBratney
(Walker Books)

Where's My Teddy? by Jez Alborough
(Walker Books)

Tickle Tickle by Helen Oxenbury
(Walker Books)

Oh Dear! by Rod Campbell
(Campbell Books)

Wacky Wild Peek A Boo by Tim Bugbird
(Make Believe Ideas Ltd)

Fuzzy Bee and Friends
(Priddy Books)

Farm Peekaboo
(DK Publishing)

Songs and rhymes are a well-tried way of communicating with babies and you can sing songs at anytime of the day with babies.

A selection of suitable songs:

Pat-a-cake
Pat a cake, pat a cake, Bakers man,
Bake me a cake as fast as you can.
Pat it and prick it and mark it with B,
And put in the oven for baby and me.
(Pat your hands during this song.)

Round and Round the Garden
Round and round the garden, like a teddy bear,
One step, two step, tickly under there
(Run your fingers across the babies palm, walk your fingers up the arm and tickle under babies arm)

Ride a Cock Horse
Ride a cock horse to Banbury Cross,
To see a fine lady upon a white horse.
With rings on her fingers and bells on her toes,
She shall have music wherever she goes.
(Bounce the baby on your knee)

This Little Piggy
This little piggy went to marker,
this little piggy stayed at home,
This little piggy had roast beef,
this little piggy had none.
This little piggy went 'wee -wee-wee'
all the way home.
(Touch each finger or toe in turn
and tickle underneath the foot or arm)

Row Row Row Your Boat
Row, row, row your boat gently down the stream
Merrily, merrily, merrily, life is but a dream.
(Face your baby, hold hands and gently move backwards and forwards)

Miss Polly Had a Dolly
Miss Polly had a dolly who was sick, sick sick,
So she phoned for the doctor to be quick, quick, quick,
The doctor came with a bag and a hat and knocked on the door with a rat a tat tat
He looked at the dolly and he shook his head and he said Miss Polly put her straight to bed
He wrote on a paper for a pill, pill, pill, I'll be back in the morning for my bill, bill, bill.
(Act out the actions to match the song.)

Twinkle, Twinkle
Twinkle, twinkle little star, how I wonder what you are
Up above the world so high, like a diamond in the sky
Twinkle, twinkle little star, how I wonder what you are.
(Use your fingers to represent a star.)

Incy Wincy Spider
Incy wincy spider climbing up the spout,
Down came the rain and washed the spider out
Out came the sunshine and dried up all the rain,
So incy wincy spider climbed the spout again
(Use your fingers to represent a spider.)

let's **talk** about

Weather

ISBN 978-1-4081-2668-4

let's **talk** about
Toys

ISBN 978-1-4081-2667-7

let's **talk** about
the Park

ISBN 978-1-4081-2669-1

let's **talk** about
Farms

ISBN 978-1-4081-2666-0

This exciting new series covers the six EYFS areas of learning and development through a variety of age appropriate themes. It fulfils the aims of the Every Child a Talker initiative.

Let's talk about... **provides practitioners and children with entertaining, exciting and stimulating language activities that foster and enhance early language learning.**